I0425930

July 2012

MORTGAGE FORECLOSURES

Regulatory Oversight of Compliance with Servicemembers Civil Relief Act Has Been Limited

GAO

Accountability ★ Integrity ★ Reliability

GAO-12-700

GAO
Accountability * Integrity * Reliability

Highlights

Highlights of GAO-12-700, a report to congressional requesters

MORTGAGE FORECLOSURES

Regulatory Oversight of Compliance with Servicemembers Civil Relief Act Has Been Limited

Why GAO Did This Study

SCRA protects servicemembers whose active duty military service prevents them from meeting financial obligations, by allowing interest rates on certain debts to be reduced and requiring a court order before certain foreclosures on their homes can occur. With foreclosures rising, reports surfaced of instances in which financial institutions failed to comply with SCRA. GAO examined the (1) eligibility for SCRA protections and extent of SCRA mortgage-related violations by depository institutions, (2) SCRA compliance oversight by prudential regulators and other federal agencies, and (3) the military services' efforts to educate servicemembers on SCRA. GAO collected data on populations eligible for SCRA from DOD and SCRA violations from banking and law enforcement agencies and reviewed a stratified random sample of prudential regulators' examinations of banks and credit unions. GAO also interviewed regulators, law enforcement and military officials, and military service organizations.

What GAO Recommends

Prudential regulators should conduct more extensive loan file testing for SCRA compliance. Regulators and other agencies that oversee mortgage activities should also explore opportunities for information sharing on SCRA compliance oversight, and VA should expand its SCRA compliance monitoring efforts. Finally, DOD and DHS should assess the effectiveness of their efforts to provide SCRA information to servicemembers. The agencies generally agreed and noted actions responsive to GAO's recommendations.

View GAO-12-700. For more information, contact Mathew Scirè at (202) 512-8678 or sciremj@gao.gov.

What GAO Found

Certain protections under the Servicemembers Civil Relief Act (SCRA) only apply to those servicemembers who obtained mortgages prior to becoming active duty, but at least 15,000 instances of financial institutions failing to properly reduce servicemembers' mortgage interest rates and over 300 improper foreclosures have been identified by federal investigations and financial institutions in recent years. Additional independent reviews of financial institutions' compliance are under way, and staff from some of these institutions told GAO that they have implemented improved practices—such as creating single points of contact familiar with military issues for borrowers—to better comply with SCRA.

Federal regulators' oversight of SCRA compliance has been limited. GAO estimates that from 2007 through 2011 prudential depository institution regulators—the Federal Deposit Insurance Corporation, Federal Reserve Board, National Credit Union Administration, and Office of the Comptroller of the Currency—reviewed 48 percent of all banks and credit unions for SCRA compliance. Of these institutions that were reviewed for SCRA compliance, only about half received examinations that involved testing of compliance by reviewing loan files. Further, GAO found that examiners had only reviewed loans identified by the institution as involving servicemembers and had not independently selected a statistical sample of loan files, which would have provided greater assurance of SCRA compliance. Without more testing, which examination and auditing guidance suggest provides increased verification, regulators are less likely to detect SCRA violations. Various other federal agencies are involved in SCRA compliance oversight. The Department of Justice has explicit SCRA enforcement authority and since 2007 has brought three cases against mortgage servicers for violations. The Department of Veterans Affairs (VA), Federal Housing Administration, and Federal Housing Finance Agency—which regulates the government-sponsored enterprises—all obtain information about SCRA compliance at the servicers that participate in the mortgage programs they administer or regulate, but the agencies and the prudential regulators do not share such information among themselves. Collaboration among these agencies could lead to more effective supervision and improve their awareness of potential problems with SCRA compliance. Further, VA oversight of mortgage servicers does not specifically review for SCRA compliance. By increasing its SCRA compliance monitoring efforts, VA could better ensure that servicemembers with VA loans are better protected.

SCRA requires that the Department of Defense (DOD) and Department of Homeland Security (DHS)—which oversees the Coast Guard—inform servicemembers of their SCRA rights. The military services provide this information in various forms, such as briefings and websites. However, some military officials said that servicemembers—particularly members of the National Guard and reserve—often receive SCRA information as part of briefings with numerous other topics prior to deployment and do not always retain the necessary awareness when they need it later. DOD and DHS do not assess the effectiveness of their SCRA education methods, such as by using focus groups of servicemembers or testing to reinforce retention of SCRA information. Without such assessment, they may not be able to ensure that they are informing servicemembers of their rights in the most effective manner.

_____ United States Government Accountability Office

Contents

Abbreviations

ABA	American Bar Association
CFPB	Consumer Financial Protection Bureau
DCI	Data collection instrument
DMDC	Defense Manpower Data Center
DOD	Department of Defense
DHS	Department of Homeland Security
HUD	Department of Housing and Urban Development
DOJ	Department of Justice
VA	Department of Veterans Affairs
FDIC	Federal Deposit Insurance Corporation
FFIEC	Federal Financial Institutions Examination Council
FHA	Federal Housing Administration
FHFA	Federal Housing Finance Agency
NCUA	National Credit Union Administration
OCC	Office of the Comptroller of the Currency
OTS	Office of Thrift Supervision
SCRA	Servicemembers Civil Relief Act

July 17, 2012

Congressional Requesters

The Servicemembers Civil Relief Act (SCRA) is intended to provide protections to servicemembers in the event that their military service prevents them from meeting financial obligations.[1] The intent of the act is to allow servicemembers to focus on their duties without having to experience difficulties in their financial affairs as a result of their service. The act provides numerous protections to servicemembers serving on active duty,[2] including prohibiting mortgage servicers—entities responsible for administering home-mortgage loans—from foreclosing on their homes without court orders, capping the interest rate and fees on their mortgages at 6 percent, and prohibiting adverse credit reporting for servicemembers who invoke their SCRA rights. In order to be eligible for some of these protections, servicemembers must have incurred their mortgage prior to their active duty service.

In addition to landmark civil cases against mortgage servicers by servicemembers, record numbers of foreclosures and allegations that mortgage servicers did not ensure that all foreclosure documents were properly signed or notarized in recent years caused federal agencies to pay increased attention to servicing activities.[3] At the end of 2010, federal bank regulators conducted reviews of foreclosure processing at 14 federally regulated mortgage servicers. These reviews identified instances in which servicemembers who were protected by SCRA had been foreclosed upon and led to numerous additional inquiries to determine the extent to which servicemembers' SCRA rights had been violated. For example, in 2011, some of the nation's largest mortgage

---

[1] 50 U.S.C. §§ 501 – 597b.

[2] Active duty for armed services is defined in 10 U.S.C. §101(d)(1) as "full-time duty in the active military service of the United States." Such terms include "full-time training duty, annual training duty, and attendance, while in the active military service, at a school designated as a service school by law or by the Secretary of the military department concerned." The act entitles servicemembers to foreclosure protection for a period of 9 months after their active duty service and to interest rate caps for up to 1 year after active duty service.

[3] *See e.g.* Hurley v. Deutsche Bank Trust Company Americas, No. 1:08-CV-361, 2009 WL 701006 (W.D. Mich. March 13, 2009).

servicers—Chase Home Finance, LLC; BAC Home Loans Servicing, LP; and Saxon Mortgage Services Inc.—settled lawsuits for millions of dollars for faulty mortgage servicing and foreclosure practices that included allegedly foreclosing on and charging excess interest and fees to servicemembers in violation of SCRA.

In response to these identified instances of SCRA violations, congressional requesters asked us to examine various aspects of federal oversight of SCRA compliance. This report discusses (1) what is known about SCRA eligibility, the number of violations that have occurred, and practices financial institutions use to comply with SCRA, (2) what oversight financial regulators and other federal agencies have taken to help ensure financial institutions' compliance with the act, and (3) actions the Department of Defense (DOD), Department of Homeland Security (DHS), Department of Veterans Affairs (VA), and others have taken to ensure that servicemembers and others are informed of protections provided under the act. As agreed with your staff, the scope of our review includes primarily SCRA protections related to servicemembers' residential mortgages.

To describe what is known about the practices financial institutions use to comply with SCRA, we interviewed representatives, from a non-generalizable sample of 4 of the 10 largest mortgage servicers based on unpaid principal balance of mortgages serviced, about their SCRA compliance practices and challenges and reviewed relevant policies and procedures. We also interviewed representatives of financial industry associations, including those that represent the mortgage industry and financial institutions with a large military customer base. We reviewed letters from 10 mortgage servicers on their SCRA compliance history and activities, which were written in response to an investigation by the U.S. House of Representatives Committee on Oversight and Government Reform. We also reviewed data on SCRA violations found during bank and credit union examinations conducted between 2007 and 2011 by the prudential depository institution regulators—the Board of Governors of the Federal Reserve System (Federal Reserve), the Federal Deposit Insurance Corporation (FDIC), the National Credit Union Administration (NCUA), and the Office of the Comptroller of the Currency (OCC)—as well as data from Department of Justice (DOJ) enforcement actions and a recent class action settlement against a large mortgage servicer.

To assess the oversight financial regulators have taken to help ensure financial institutions' compliance with SCRA, we reviewed prudential regulators' examination policies and procedures and interviewed officials from these agencies. To assess the extent to which prudential regulators examined banks and credit unions for SCRA compliance, we selected a stratified random sample of 160 depository institutions (40 from each of the four prudential regulators) and reviewed the workpapers for each of the examinations from 2007 through 2011 for 152 of these institutions.[4] Our sample included only institutions that hold mortgages in their loan portfolios and service those loans themselves or institutions that service mortgages for other institutions. We analyzed the examination workpapers to estimate the percentage of institutions for which prudential regulators conducted SCRA compliance reviews and determine the frequencies with which different examination procedures were used for these reviews.[5] To describe the SCRA oversight activities of other federal agencies, we reviewed SCRA oversight policies and procedures for DOJ, the Federal Housing Administration (FHA), government-sponsored enterprises (the enterprises)—Fannie Mae and Freddie Mac—and VA. We reviewed SCRA cases DOJ settled from 2007 through 2011 and SCRA compliance oversight policies and procedures of FHA, Fannie Mae, Freddie Mac, and VA, and we interviewed officials from these agencies.

To determine what actions DOD, DHS, VA, and others have taken to ensure servicemembers are informed of their SCRA rights, we reviewed the act to determine what it requires agencies to do and interviewed two SCRA experts. We also reviewed DOD and DHS policies and procedures and interviewed officials from DOD's Office of Legal Policy, DHS, and the National Guard Bureau. To determine what actions other agencies, including VA, Consumer Financial Protection Bureau (CFPB), and FHA, were taking to inform servicemembers and others of SCRA protections, we reviewed notifications they provide to mortgage servicers on SCRA compliance and interviewed officials at these agencies. To determine how servicemembers learn about their SCRA protections and what challenges

---

[4]Eight of the selected institutions were excluded from our analysis. Three institutions regulated by the Federal Reserve were excluded because they were recently chartered and therefore had not had an examination. We also excluded five credit unions because they were state chartered, meaning that state supervisory authorities and not NCUA served as the primary regulator for these institutions. See appendix I for additional information about our sample.

[5]Estimates based on this workpaper review are subject to sampling error. All estimates used in this report are presented along with their 95 percent confidence intervals. See appendix I for additional information about our sample.

they face asserting those protections, we selected six military installation legal assistance offices (one for the Army, Navy, Marine Corps, and Coast Guard and two for the Air Force) based on a geographic distribution of states with high numbers of foreclosures and large active duty and reservist populations, and interviewed the legal assistance attorneys who work directly with servicemembers who visit these offices. We reviewed examples of SCRA training and outreach that these offices develop and distribute to servicemembers. We also interviewed two legal assistance attorneys from the reserve components who were recommended during our interviews with legal assistance attorneys, as well as representatives from seven military servicemember groups that were selected based on their broad representation of servicemembers. See appendix I for more information on our objectives, scope, and methodology.

We conducted this performance audit from August 2011 to July 2012 in accordance with generally accepted government auditing standards. Those standards require that we plan and perform the audit to obtain sufficient, appropriate evidence to provide a reasonable basis for our findings and conclusions based on our audit objectives. We believe that the evidence obtained provides a reasonable basis for our findings and conclusions based on our audit objectives.

Background

Congress passed the Soldiers' and Sailors' Civil Relief Act in 1940 to provide servicemembers protections to help them meet the unique circumstances they face when serving their country.[6] In response to the increased use of Reserve and National Guard military units in the Global War on Terrorism, Congress enacted SCRA in December 2003 as a modernized version of the Soldiers' and Sailors' Civil Relief Act. In addition to providing protections related to residential mortgages, the act covers other types of loans, such as credit card and automobile and a variety of other issues, such as rental agreements, eviction, installment

---

[6]A prior version of the law was enacted in 1918.

contracts, civil judicial and administrative proceedings, motor vehicle leases, life insurance, health insurance, and income tax payments.[7]

SCRA provides the following mortgage-related protections to servicemembers:[8]

- *Interest Rate Cap.* Servicemembers who obtain mortgages prior to serving on active duty status are eligible to have their interest rate capped at 6 percent for the duration of their active duty status and for 12 months after returning from active duty service.[9] Interest above 6 percent is to be forgiven by the servicer. Servicemembers are required to inform their servicer of their active duty status in order to avail themselves of this provision.

- *Foreclosure Proceedings.* A servicer cannot sell, foreclose, or seize the property of a servicemember for breach of a pre-service obligation unless a court order is issued prior to the foreclosure on the

---

[7]A servicemember may waive many of the rights and protections provided by SCRA provided the waiver meets certain criteria, including that it is in writing and is in a document separate from the obligation or liability to which it applies. 50 U.S.C. § 517. The waiver provision "is designed to induce servicemembers and their creditors to adjust their respective rights privately and to make it clear that no restrictions have been placed upon the usual right of the parties to re-negotiate an obligation." The Judge Advocate General's Legal Center & School, U.S. Army, JA 260, *Servicemembers Civil Relief Act*, 2-8 (March 2006).

[8]SCRA defines servicemembers as members of the uniformed services found in 10 U.S.C. §101(a)(5) which includes the commissioned corps of the National Oceanic and Atmospheric Administration and the Public Health Service. Active duty is defined in 10 U.S.C. §101(d)(1). We did not collect any specific information related to SCRA protections for officials from the National Oceanic and Atmospheric Administration and the Public Health Service for this report.

[9]50 U.S.C. app. §527. The act defines interest to include service charges, renewal charges, fees, or any other charges (except bona fide insurance). A servicer has the right to challenge the reduction in interest in court, if it believes that the servicemember's ability to pay interest above 6 percent is "not materially affected by reason of the servicemember's military service." 50 U.S.C. § 527(c).

property.[10] This protection is effective until 9 months after the term of active duty service ends.[11] If the servicer files an action in court to enforce the terms of the mortgage, the court may stay any proceedings or adjust the obligation to preserve the interests of the parties.

- *Mortgage prepayment penalties.* A court may decide that servicemembers who have mortgages that impose penalties for paying off the balance early are not subject to these penalties if the servicemember incurs such fees due to military service and the ability of the servicemember to pay the fees is materially affected by military service.[12] For example, a servicemember who receives a permanent change-of-station order to relocate to another area may receive a court order that waives the penalty for selling his or her home and paying off the mortgage early.

- *Adverse credit reporting protections.* A servicer may not report adverse credit information to a credit reporting agency solely because a servicemember exercises his or her SCRA rights, including a request to have his or her mortgage interest rate and fees be capped at 6 percent.[13]

---

[10]50 U.S.C. app. § 533(c). This provision is directed at foreclosures that are referred to as non-judicial. Once a mortgage servicer decides to foreclose, it follows either a judicial or non-judicial foreclosure method, depending on state law. In a judicial foreclosure, servicers initiate a formal foreclosure action by filing a lawsuit in court. The presiding judge, upon the conclusion of a hearing, will, in the appropriate circumstances, issue an order for the foreclosure to proceed. By contrast, a non-judicial foreclosure process takes place outside the courtroom and is typically conducted by the trustee named in the deed-of-trust document. Trustees, and sometimes servicers, generally send a notice of default to the borrower and publish a notice of sale in area newspapers or legal publications. Pursuant to 50 U.S.C. § 533(c), if a lender in a non-judicial foreclosure state forecloses on a servicemember that took out his or her mortgage prior to active duty service without a court order, the foreclosure is invalid.

[11]In 2008, P. L. 110-289, § 2203, extended this protection for servicemembers from 90 days after active duty service to 9 months after active duty service, effective until December 31, 2010. In 2010, P. L. 111-346, § 2 changed the expiration date of the 9-month protection to December 31, 2012; on January 1, 2013, the period prohibiting foreclosure without a court order will revert to 90 days.

[12]50 U.S.C. app. §523(b).

[13]50 U.S.C. app §518.

GAO-12-700 Mortgage Foreclosures

In addition to SCRA, the Housing and Urban Development Act of 1968 includes a requirement applicable to institutions that service mortgages. This act requires that all mortgage servicers that service home loans provide notification of the availability of homeownership counseling offered by the lender to eligible homeowners who fail to pay any amount by the due date.[14] In 2006, changes were made to the homeownership counseling notice requirement. Mortgage servicers are required to alert borrowers of SCRA protections if they are in default on their mortgage, and the notice instructs borrowers to notify their servicer if they believe they are eligible for SCRA protections.[15] Servicers must provide the notification within 45 days from the date a payment was missed by a borrower. The Department of Housing and Urban Development (HUD) developed and disseminated the format for this notice.

SCRA provides protections to active duty servicemembers in all five of the military services—Army, Navy, Air Force, Marine Corps, and Coast Guard—as well as members of each of these services' reserve component.[16] These components include the Army Reserve, Navy Reserve, Marine Corps Reserve, Air Force Reserve, Coast Guard Reserve, Army National Guard, and Air National Guard.[17] In 2010, active

---

[14] Section 106(c)(5) of the Housing and Urban Development Act of 1968 (12 U.S.C. 1701x (c)(5)). ("Home loan" means a loan secured by a mortgage or lien on residential property. A homeowner is eligible for counseling if (1) the loan is secured by the homeowner's principal residence, (2) the home loan is not assisted by the U.S. Department of Agriculture's Rural Housing Service, and (3) the homeowner is, or is expected to be, unable to make payments, correct a home loan delinquency within a reasonable time, or resume full home loan payments due to a reduction in the homeowner's income. In lieu of providing notification of available homeownership counseling offered by the lender, servicers may provide either a list of HUD-approved nonprofit homeownership counseling organizations or the toll-free number HUD has established through which a list of such organizations can be obtained.)

[15] Section 688 of the National Defense Authorization Act for Fiscal Year 2006 (Public Law 109-163, enacted January 6, 2006) amended the required content of notifications of homeownership counseling availability under §106(c)(5)(A)(ii) of the Housing and Urban Development Act (12 U.S.C. 1701x(c)(5)(A)(ii)) and directed HUD to develop and disseminate a format for the required notice.

[16] DHS oversees servicemembers in the Coast Guard and the Coast Guard Reserve.

[17] The reserve components consist of three categories: Ready Reserve, Standby Reserve, and Retired Reserve. The Ready Reserve is comprised of the Selected Reserve, the Individual Ready Reserve, and the Inactive National Guard. Because Selected Reserve members train throughout the year and participate annually in active duty training exercises, our report discusses this category of the reserve.

duty servicemembers comprised 63 percent of the military's force, and the reserve components represented the remaining 37 percent of the military force.[18] Figure 1 shows the distribution of the military population and shows that the Army constitutes the greatest percentage of both active duty servicemembers and the reserve forces.

Figure 1: U.S. Military Population, 2010

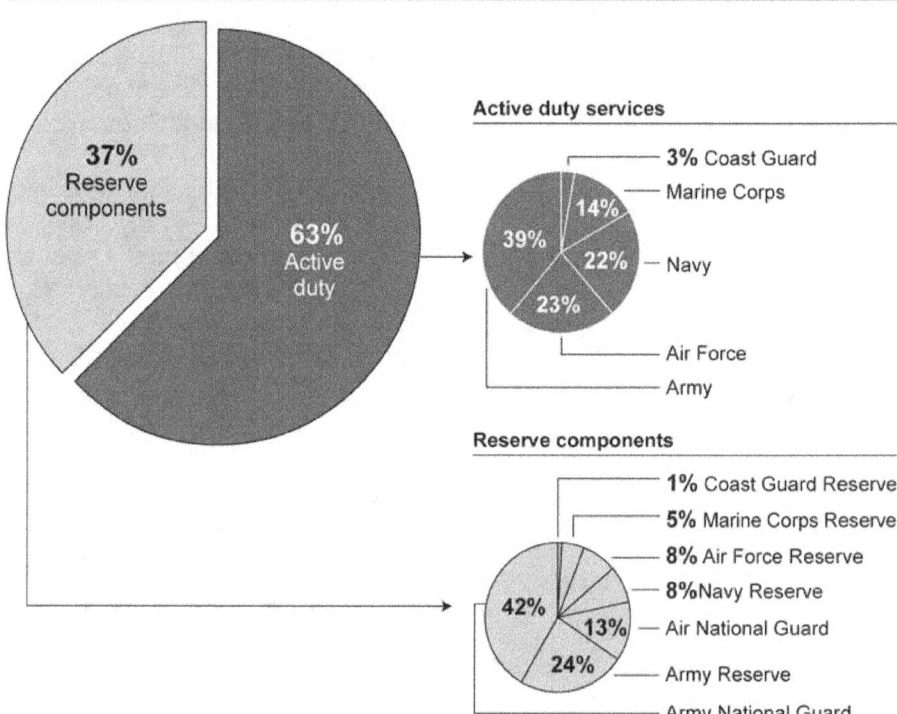

Source: GAO analysis of *Demographics 2010: Profile of the Military Community.*

Note: Data on the reserve components represent only the Selected Reserve within the Ready Reserve.

While the Army Reserve, the Navy Reserve, the Marine Corps Reserve, and the Air Force Reserve are federal entities, the Army National Guard and the Air National Guard (known collectively as the National Guard)

---

[18]The data on the reserve components represent only those of the Selected Reserve.

have both federal and state missions.[19] Members of the National Guard who are eligible for SCRA protections are those who have been called into federal active duty service.[20] In addition, members of the National Guard recalled for state duty are also eligible for SCRA protections under certain circumstances.[21]

The responsibility of extending mortgage-related SCRA protections to eligible servicemembers often falls to mortgage servicers. While some institutions that originate home mortgage loans hold the loans as assets on their balance sheets, institutions generally sell them to other financial institutions or the enterprises—Fannie Mae or Freddie Mac. The enterprises purchase mortgages from primary mortgage lenders. They hold some of the mortgages they purchase in their portfolios, but they package the majority into mortgage-backed securities and sell them to investors in the secondary mortgage market. The enterprises guarantee these investors the timely payment of principal and interest. If a mortgage originator sells its loans to either an investor or to an institution that securitizes them, another financial institution or other entity is appointed as the mortgage servicer to manage payment collections and other activities associated with these loans. Mortgage servicers, which can be large mortgage finance companies, commercial banks, or small specialty companies unaffiliated with a larger financial institution, earn a fee for duties they perform, such as sending borrowers monthly account statements, answering customer-service inquiries, collecting monthly mortgage payments, maintaining escrow accounts for property taxes and hazard insurance, and forwarding proper payments to the mortgage owners. Other mortgage lenders that hold the mortgages they originate may service the loans internally or outsource this function.

---

[19]The National Guard is comprised of 54 separate organizations: one for each state, and one each for Puerto Rico, Guam, the U.S. Virgin Islands, and the District of Columbia.

[20]Members of the National Guard who are called to federal active duty service are under Title 10 of the United States Code. When under the command of their respective governors, National Guard members operate under Title 32 status and may be called upon to carry out a number of domestic missions, such as responding to natural disasters, protecting state assets from terrorist attack, and training for their federal missions.

[21]National Guard members are eligible for SCRA protections when called to state active duty under 32 U.S.C. § 502(f) if the duty is because of a federal emergency, the request is made by the President or the Secretary of Defense, and the member is activated for longer than 30 days. 50 U.S.C. app. § 511(2)(A)(ii). An example of National Guard members fitting into this category would be those members activated by the states, at the request of the President, to provide airport security after the 9-11 attacks.

In the event that a borrower becomes delinquent on loan payments, the mortgage servicer must decide whether to pursue a home retention workout or foreclosure alternative, such as a short sale, or proceed with foreclosure. If the mortgage servicer determines that foreclosure is the most appropriate option, it follows one of two foreclosure methods, depending on state law. In a judicial foreclosure, a judge presides over the process in a court proceeding. Mortgage servicers initiate a formal foreclosure action by filing a lawsuit with a court. A nonjudicial foreclosure process takes place outside the courtroom and is typically conducted by a trustee named in the deed-of-trust document that accompanied the mortgage. Trustees, and sometimes mortgage servicers, generally send a notice of default to the borrower and publish a notice of sale in area newspapers or legal publications.

Prudential regulators—FDIC, Federal Reserve, NCUA, and OCC—have the authority to conduct reviews of any aspect of banks' activities, including compliance with applicable consumer protection laws, such as SCRA.[22] OCC charters and supervises national banks and federal thrifts. The Federal Reserve supervises state-chartered banks that opt to be members of the Federal Reserve System, bank holding companies, thrift holding companies, and the nondepository institution subsidiaries of those institutions. FDIC supervises FDIC-insured state-chartered banks that are not members of the Federal Reserve System, as well as federally insured state savings banks and thrifts. NCUA charters and supervises federally chartered credit unions and insures savings in federal and most state-chartered credit unions.[23] OCC regulates the vast majority of mortgage servicing in the United States. For example, OCC-regulated servicers accounted for close to 80 percent of the unpaid principal balance on serviced mortgages in the third quarter of 2011. The prudential regulators conduct risk-based examinations of the institutions they oversee on a routine basis. Because examinations are risk-based and there are a

---

[22]12 U.S.C. §1818; 12 U.S.C. §1786.

[23]The Dodd-Frank Wall Street Reform and Consumer Protection Act, Pub. L. No. 111-203, 124 Stat. 1376 (2010), eliminated the Office of Thrift Supervision (OTS), which chartered and supervised federally chartered savings institutions and savings and loan holding companies. Supervisory authority was transferred to OCC for federal savings associations, to FDIC for state savings associations, and to the Federal Reserve for savings and loan holding companies and their subsidiaries, other than depository institutions. The transfer of these powers was completed on July 21, 2011, and OTS was officially dissolved 90 days later.

number of consumer compliance laws for which examiners assess compliance during an examination, SCRA compliance is not assessed during every examination.

The Dodd-Frank Wall Street Reform and Consumer Protection Act (Dodd-Frank Act) established CFPB and provided it with the authority to regulate mortgage servicers with respect to federal consumer financial law.[24] Consumer financial protection functions from seven existing federal agencies were transferred to the new agency.[25] For mortgage servicers that are depository institutions with more than $10 billion in assets or their affiliates, CFPB will have exclusive supervisory authority and primary enforcement authority to ensure compliance with federal consumer financial law.[26] Additionally, if a mortgage servicer is a nondepository institution, CFPB will have both supervisory and enforcement authority to ensure compliance with federal consumer financial law.[27] Finally, CFPB will have rulemaking authority with respect to mortgage servicers, including authority that transfers from other federal agencies such as the Federal Reserve and the Federal Trade Commission.[28] SCRA, however, was not one of the enumerated laws for which oversight transferred to CFPB. The prudential regulators remain responsible for overseeing compliance with the law for any of the entities they supervise that are servicing mortgages.

Other federal agencies are involved in the mortgage market by operating mortgage programs aimed at expanding homeownership for populations who may encounter difficulties in obtaining mortgages. For example, FHA

---

[24]Federal consumer financial law is a defined term in the Dodd-Frank Act that includes over a dozen existing federal consumer protection laws, including the Truth in Lending Act, the Real Estate Settlement Procedures Act, and the Equal Credit Opportunity Act, as well as the provisions of title X of the Dodd-Frank Act itself. 12 U.S.C. § 5481(12), (14).

[25]The seven agencies are the Federal Reserve, FDIC, Federal Trade Commission, NCUA, OCC, OTS, and HUD.

[26]12 U.S.C. § 5515.

[27]CFPB's nondepository supervision authorities specifically extend to any covered person that "offers or provides origination, brokerage or servicing of loans secured by real estate for use by consumers primarily for personal, family or household purposes, or loan modification or foreclosure relief services in connection with such loans." 12 U.S.C. § 5514(a)(1)(A).

[28]12 U.S.C. § 5512. The Federal Trade Commission will retain its current enforcement authority.

has played a large role in assisting minority, lower-income, and first-time homebuyers in obtaining mortgages. FHA's program insures private lenders against losses from borrower defaults on mortgages that meet FHA criteria for properties with one to four housing units. As of September 2011, almost 3,700 lending institutions were approved to participate in FHA's mortgage insurance programs for single-family homes. FHA also offers special protections for servicemembers who have FHA-insured loans. For example, FHA-approved lenders are authorized to postpone principal payments and foreclosure proceedings for servicemembers on active duty who have FHA-insured mortgages.[29]

VA is also active in the mortgage market through its Home Loan Guaranty program, which provides lenders a guaranty on a portion of mortgage loans for eligible veterans, active duty servicemembers, surviving spouses, and members of the reserve components in recognition of their service. According to VA, the program operates by substituting the federal government's guaranty for a down payment that might otherwise be required. VA guarantees a portion of the mortgage loan in the event that borrowers default, providing lenders with substantial financial protections against some of the losses that may be associated with extending such mortgage loans. In 2011, VA guaranteed over 350,000 loans to veteran borrowers.

The Housing and Economic Recovery Act of 2008 created the Federal Housing Finance Agency (FHFA) and gave it responsibility for, among other things, the supervision and regulation of the housing-related enterprises: Fannie Mae, Freddie Mac, and the 12 federal home loan banks.[30] Specifically, FHFA was assigned responsibility for ensuring that each of the regulated entities operates in a safe and sound manner, including maintenance of adequate capital and internal controls, and carries out its housing and community development finance mission. FHFA has no direct authority over mortgage servicers, but does have authority to ensure that the housing enterprises are being run safely and soundly, as well as the power to impose operational, managerial, and internal control standards on the companies.

---

[29]24 CFR 203.610, 24 CFR 203.345 and 203.346.

[30]Pub. L. 110-289, sec. 1101.

SCRA Eligibility, Violations, and Compliance

SCRA Requirements Limit Eligibility for Mortgage Protections

The total number of servicemembers eligible for the mortgage protections provided by SCRA is not known, but the size of this population is likely limited because the act provides protections only to servicemembers who meet certain eligibility requirements. The maximum number of servicemembers potentially eligible for mortgage protections under SCRA at any one time includes those servicemembers on active duty service and those who have recently left it.[31] According to DOD, between 2007 and 2010 about 2 million servicemembers, including those activated from the reserve components, were on active duty.[32] However, the number of servicemembers who may actually qualify for the SCRA mortgage protections is a smaller portion of this population because some of the act's protections only extend to servicemembers who obtained their mortgages prior to entering active duty service or servicemembers whose military service materially affects their ability to pay their mortgage. However, representatives from all the mortgage servicers with whom we spoke stated that they do not assess whether a servicemember's ability to pay has been materially affected by their active duty status and that they provide eligible servicemembers SCRA protections regardless of whether their ability to pay is materially affected or not.

According to DOD officials, representatives from industry trade groups, SCRA experts, and military service organizations, the servicemembers most likely to be eligible for SCRA mortgage protections are members of the reserve components. These servicemembers are more likely to have had mortgages prior to entering active duty service and some may potentially experience a decline in their incomes as they leave their civilian employment and begin receiving their military pay. We have

---

[31]Reserve personnel are entitled to most of SCRA's protections on the date they receive active duty orders. 50 U.S.C. App. § 516(a).

[32]Because some members of the reserve components may have been activated more than once between 2007 and 2010, this estimate may represent a larger population of servicemembers than those that were eligible for SCRA mortgage protections during this period.

previously reported, however that servicemembers belonging to the reserve components on average earn more income while activated.[33] According to DOD officials, the number of servicemembers activated from the reserve components from 2007 through 2010 was approximately 576,500.

The maximum number of servicemembers who are eligible for SCRA mortgage protections is also a smaller portion of the total military population because many do not own homes for which they have taken out mortgage loans. According to the Census Bureau, the U.S. homeownership rate was about 67 percent in 2010. However, research shows that servicemembers are generally less likely to own their own homes.[34] For example, according to DOD's 2008 annual Status of Forces surveys—surveys that DOD sends annually to active duty servicemembers and members of the reserve components to evaluate various programs and policies and their impact on servicemembers—only 34 percent of active duty servicemembers and 55 percent of reserve component servicemembers reported that they owned or made mortgage payments on a home in the previous 12 months.[35] However, even those military families who have mortgages may not be eligible for SCRA protections. First, some SCRA mortgage protections only apply to servicemembers who took out their mortgage before being placed on active duty. Also, given that mortgage interest rates have been at historic lows in recent years, servicemembers who took out mortgage loans during this period before being placed on active duty may be likely to have loans with rates lower than the SCRA-mandated level of 6 percent.

---

[33]GAO, *Military Personnel: Reserve Component Servicemembers On Average Earn More Income while Activated*, GAO-09-688R (Washington, D.C.: June 23, 2009), p.3.

[34]Census computes the homeownership rate by dividing the number of owner-occupied housing units by the number of occupied housing units or households.

[35]DOD *Status of Forces Survey of Active Duty Members* (August 2008) and *Status of Forces Survey of Reserve Component Members* (November 2008). The margin of error for active duty servicemembers is plus or minus 1 percent and plus or minus 2 percent for reserve component members. Survey results do not include responses from members of the Coast Guard and Coast Guard Reserve.

Thousands of Mortgage-Related SCRA Violations Have Been Identified to Date

Although the total number of SCRA violations is not known, thousands of SCRA violations have been identified from a number of sources. First, DOJ—which is responsible for enforcing SCRA—settled investigations in 2011 with two mortgage servicers and identified 165 instances of active duty servicemembers who had their homes foreclosed upon without the mortgage servicer seeking the proper court order as required by the act.[36] Second, in July 2011, as part of its investigation into SCRA violations, the U.S. House of Representatives Committee on Oversight and Government Reform sent letters to 10 large mortgage servicers requesting them to identify the total number of improper foreclosures and interest-rate and fee violations they had committed. In their responses, 6 mortgage servicers reported having conducted a total of at least 148 improper foreclosures against servicemembers and failing to reduce interest rates or fees on the mortgages for over 14,000 servicemembers since 2005. Third, as the result of a class-action lawsuit filed by several servicemembers, as of January 2012, Chase Home Finance, LLC had issued refunds to approximately 13,500 borrowers for interest and fees charged in excess of SCRA protections since 2005.[37] Many of the mortgage servicers involved in these investigations are among the largest in the industry and service millions of loans. Table 1 summarizes the various SCRA violations identified by these sources to date.

---

[36]United States of America v. BAC Home Loans Servicing, Civil No. 2:11-cv-04534-PA-MRW (C.D. Cal. 2011) and United States of America v. Saxon Mortgage Services, Inc., Civil No. 3:11-cv-0111-F (N.D. Tex. 2011). BAC Home Loans Servicing, LP, was formerly known as Countrywide Home Loans Servicing and is a subsidiary of Bank of America Corporation. Saxon Mortgage Services was a subsidiary of Morgan Stanley.

[37]Rowles v. Chase Home Finance, Civil No. 9:10-cv-01756-MBS (D.S.C. 2011).

Table 1: Violations of SCRA Mortgage Protections Identified through Various Reviews

Mortgage servicer	Source of data	Period in review	Number of improper SCRA foreclosures identified	Number of instances in which interest rates and fees charged were not reduced
BAC Home Loans Servicing	DOJ	Jan. 2006–May 2009	143	Not specified
Wells Fargo	Self-reported	Foreclosure – Jan. 2006–June 2010 Interest rate and fees–Jan. 2006–June 2011	17	3,224
JPMorgan Chase	Self-reported	Jan. 2005–July 2011	54	10,000
	Class action settlement	Jan. 2005–Jan 2012	Not specified	13,500
Citi	Self-reported	Foreclosure– Jan. 2007–June 2011 Interest rate and fees–Jan. 2006–June 2011	0	140
Ally Financial	Self-reported	Not specified	77	923
PHH Mortgage	Self-reported	Jan. 2006–June 2011	0	304
SunTrust Mortgage	Self-reported	Not specified	0	2
Saxon Mortgage Services, Inc.	DOJ	Jan. 2006–Dec. 2010	22	Not specified

Source: GAO analysis of DOJ complaints and mortgage servicers' responses to House Committee on Oversight and Government Reform requests.

Through their compliance examinations, prudential regulators identified 251 instances of SCRA compliance problems at depository institutions between 2007 and 2011. FDIC identified the vast majority—230—of these issues, with Federal Reserve staff identifying 16, OCC staff identifying 4, and NCUA staff identifying 1 instance. However, these SCRA compliance issues may not specifically concern mortgages—for example, they may have involved non-mortgage-loan products, such as credit card loans.

A more complete picture of the extent of SCRA violations may result from three large-scale federal agency reviews that are ongoing. Recent enforcement actions taken by DOJ, Federal Reserve, and OCC require mortgage servicers to conduct historical reviews of their mortgage loan files to determine if servicemembers who were eligible for the SCRA mortgage protections received them, among other things. If violations are identified, the mortgage servicers are required to provide compensation to the servicemembers. Appendix II contains a detailed explanation of these reviews.

In the wake of identified SCRA violations, some mortgage servicers have implemented procedures to enhance their compliance with SCRA. Some large mortgage servicers have instituted several military status checks during the foreclosure process. For example, one large mortgage servicer now requires its foreclosure counsel to check a customer's military status prior to the initiation of foreclosure proceedings, 1 week prior to a foreclosure sale, and 1 day prior to the scheduled sale date. Some mortgage servicers have also created dedicated customer service support for military servicemembers, including telephone hotlines and websites. For example, representatives from one mortgage servicer told us that they had developed a dedicated team that is staffed with former servicemembers to assist customers with SCRA requests. These customer-support representatives also receive training on military financial issues and serve as the points of contact for any problems with delinquency, remediation, and foreclosure.

Finally, as a result of identified violations and SCRA investigations, some servicemembers will be receiving SCRA protections that go beyond those stated in the act. For example, three mortgage servicers that responded to the House Committee on Oversight and Government Reform letters noted that they have reduced the interest rate they charge on servicemembers' mortgages to 4 percent—which is below the 6 percent required in SCRA. Additionally, the National Mortgage Settlement between the federal government, 49 state attorneys general, and five large mortgage servicers that occurred in February 2012 requires the five mortgage servicers to implement new mortgage servicing standards. These new standards expand protections to certain servicemember customers of these five mortgage servicers beyond those provided in SCRA. For example, the new standards extend foreclosure protections to any servicemember—regardless of whether their mortgage was obtained prior to active duty status—who is receiving Hostile Fire/Imminent Danger Pay or is serving at a location more than 750 miles away from their home. This means that any servicemember meeting these conditions and living in a nonjudicial state who obtained a mortgage after obtaining active duty status could not be foreclosed upon without a court order. More information on the National Mortgage Settlement is contained in appendix II.

Mortgage Servicers and Others Cited Challenges to Complying with SCRA

Representatives from some mortgage servicers and industry associations cited challenges that make complying with SCRA difficult. First, mortgage servicers may not know at the time a mortgage is originated whether a borrower will be eligible for SCRA protections in the future. For example, a borrower would become eligible for SCRA mortgage protections after obtaining his or her mortgage by joining the active duty military or being called into active duty service while serving as a member of the reserve components. Therefore, mortgage servicers may not be able to flag loans at origination that could potentially become eligible for SCRA protections at a later date. Second, representatives from some mortgage servicers and industry associations also noted that military orders, which servicemembers must provide to their mortgage servicers in order to receive the SCRA interest rate protection, can be difficult to interpret. In particular, a representative from one mortgage servicer noted that the orders do not always clearly specify the start and end dates of active duty service and that the format and content of these orders can vary considerably across services, which may lead to mistakes by mortgage servicer personnel responsible for determining eligibility. Further, a DOD official explained that in some instances, military orders may not be available in a timely manner. For example, he stated that members of the reserve components may be alerted that their unit is being mobilized on a certain date; however, the servicemembers may not get the actual military orders until weeks later. This delay could lead to problems for both a servicemember and a mortgage servicer. For example, if a servicemember has been deployed, he or she may encounter difficulties sending orders to his or her mortgage servicer. Without the orders, a mortgage servicer may encounter difficulties verifying the servicemember's active duty start date in order to appropriately adjust their payment amounts.

One of the primary tools mortgage servicers use to comply with SCRA is a website operated by DOD's Defense Manpower Data Center (DMDC) that allows mortgage servicers and others to query DMDC's database to determine the active duty status of a servicemember. DMDC collects, archives, and maintains DOD personnel data. Representatives from mortgage servicers indicated that they use this website to confirm if a borrower is an active duty servicemember and may be eligible for SCRA protections and that they rely on the site to confirm if a servicemember is on active duty status prior to conducting a foreclosure. Representatives from one mortgage servicer also noted that they use the website to confirm the period of time that borrowers are eligible for the SCRA interest rate protections. The website is an important compliance tool because servicemembers are eligible for the foreclosure protections even if they do not notify their mortgage servicers that they are serving on active duty.

However, many representatives from mortgage servicers and industry associations with whom we spoke cited challenges with the usability of the website. Moreover, confusion appears to exist in the mortgage servicing industry about the availability of information in the database. For example, prior to April 2012, the website only allowed mortgage servicers to inquire about borrowers' active duty status one individual at a time. The inability to test large numbers of borrowers simultaneously—known as batch testing—made confirming borrowers' SCRA eligibility difficult given the large volumes of mortgages that some institutions service. Representatives from some mortgage servicers also indicated that sometimes the personnel information available from DMDC is not complete or accurate and that the database may produce a false-negative result. That is, it will indicate that servicemembers were not on active duty status when in fact they were. DMDC officials explained that information contained in the database depends on information provided to DMDC by the various services. Therefore, if a service has not reported a servicemember to DMDC as being on active duty status, the database will report that the servicemember is not on active duty. Additionally, representatives from mortgage servicers told us that they believe some servicemembers are not listed in the database. For example, one explained that, in some instances they have received orders from servicemembers, but when they query the database to confirm the active duty status, the servicemembers are not listed as on active duty. Other mortgage servicer representatives believed that some servicemembers may not be listed in the database for national security reasons, such as those serving in the Special Forces. However, DMDC officials told us that active duty status is updated for all servicemembers, including those on special operations.

To help address these challenges, DOD is working with the mortgage servicing industry and industry associations to improve both the usability of the website and the readability of military orders. First, to aid mortgage servicers' ability to query the database, DMDC has developed and implemented a way for mortgage servicers and others to conduct batch queries of the database from the website for up to 250,000 servicemembers at a time.[38] DOD officials also noted that they are trying to develop the capability of the database to query historical information and also to distinguish between those active duty periods for servicemembers in the National Guard that provide SCRA protections and those that do not.

Second, DOD has collaborated with the financial industry through the Financial Services Roundtable's Housing Policy Council—a consortium of financial institutions that provide mortgage credit—to develop an alternative military order form that servicemembers can attach to or provide in lieu of their military orders when requesting relief under SCRA from their mortgage servicers. This form is intended to be easier for mortgage servicers to interpret as it is shorter and more standardized than official orders, which can vary by service. According to DOD officials, this alternative form was approved by DOD in December 2011 and has been distributed to the military services as well as to financial institutions and is being used by servicemembers.

Federal Regulators' Oversight of SCRA Compliance Has Been Limited

Prudential Regulators Examine for SCRA Compliance Based on Risk Factors

Prudential regulators—FDIC, Federal Reserve, NCUA, and OCC—are responsible for supervising depository institutions' compliance with various federal consumer laws including SCRA. Consumer compliance examinations are one of the primary tools regulators use to assess this compliance. Prudential regulators all use a risk-based approach to consumer compliance examinations to determine which areas to target, with areas of higher risk receiving greater focus during examinations. For example, according to the FDIC consumer compliance examination

---

[38]DMDC made changes to the website in April 2012. These changes removed the data field on active duty start date from search results. However, according to a representative of a large mortgage servicer, it used that field to determine if servicemembers obtained their mortgages prior to active duty status. In May 2012, DMDC announced that this field would again be made available from database queries.

manual, riskier areas may include ones that involve regulatory changes or complex products. Regulatory officials also told us that because of this risk-based approach, SCRA may not be included or fully addressed within the scope of an examination. For example, officials from one regulator told us that when deciding to include SCRA in an examination they may consider, among other things, consumer complaints, internal audit results of the institution's compliance management system, and problems raised in the media. Regulators also use the risk-based approach to determine the specific examination procedures they use to assess compliance. Areas of higher risk would be subject to more extensive review procedures, while areas of lower risk would receive less extensive review. For example, according to OCC's examination manual, areas of greater risk may involve more extensive testing of loan transactions for compliance.

In 2009, the regulators developed interagency examination procedures related to SCRA through the Federal Financial Institutions Examination Council (FFIEC), including a specific checklist that examiners can use in their examinations.[39] The interagency SCRA procedures and checklist indicate that examiners should determine whether depository institutions applied and properly calculated interest-rate reductions, whether any foreclosures were conducted without a court order, and whether any servicemember requests for SCRA protection were inappropriately reported as adverse information to a credit reporting agency. Additionally, the interagency procedures suggest, among other things, that examiners (1) consider reviewing SCRA policies, procedures, and account documentation when assessing the adequacy of the institution's internal controls and (2) review whether the depository institution's compliance reviews and audit materials include transaction testing of samples covering relevant product types. The checklist contains a series of questions related to different sections of SCRA, including the ones that apply to residential mortgages.

In addition to routine risk-based consumer compliance examinations, prudential regulators conduct targeted reviews of areas of high concern.

---

[39]FFIEC is an interagency body that prescribes uniform principles, standards, and report forms for depository institution examinations. Its members currently include CFPB, FDIC, Federal Reserve, NCUA, and OCC. A representative state regulator also serves as a voting member of FFIEC. SCRA was not one of the enumerated laws under the Dodd-Frank Act for which oversight transferred to CFPB.

For example, FDIC, Federal Reserve, and OCC conducted an interagency review of the foreclosure policies and practices of 14 mortgage servicers in late 2010, in response to the large number of foreclosures since 2007 and continued weaknesses in the mortgage market. The examiners evaluated the adequacy of each mortgage servicer's operating procedures and controls and preparation of foreclosure documentation, among other things. Although the interagency review was not intended to directly assess SCRA compliance, during the course of this effort, two mortgage servicers nonetheless identified SCRA compliance problems.[40] Additionally, in June 2011, OCC issued guidance to all of its regulated institutions that required them to conduct self-assessments of their foreclosure management practices. OCC examiners will review the self-assessments in the subsequent examination of the institutions.[41]

Oversight of SCRA Compliance Varied by Institution, Year, and Regulator

The extent to which SCRA was reviewed varied by the size of the depository institution, the year in which the examination took place, and the regulator that conducted the examination from 2007 through 2011. Based on our review, we estimate that from 2007 through 2011, prudential regulators reviewed SCRA compliance in at least one examination for 48 percent of all the institutions they oversaw that serviced mortgages.[42] This estimate includes documentation of an SCRA review for any type of loan product (e.g., residential mortgage, credit card, automobile, and other types of products). Some of the reasons bank examiners cited for including SCRA in the scope of an examination

---

[40]GAO, *Mortgage Foreclosures: Documentation Problems Reveal Need for Ongoing Regulatory Oversight*, GAO-11-433 (Washington, D.C.: May 2, 2011), p.28.

[41]The prudential regulators and others recently took steps intended to address mortgage servicer practices that may pose risk to homeowners serving in the military. In June 2012, FDIC, Federal Reserve, OCC, NCUA, and CFPB issued joint guidance to mortgage servicers regarding servicemembers with permanent change-of-station orders. Because such physical relocations can affect servicemembers' ability to pay their mortgages, the guidance states that mortgage servicers should ensure that their employees are adequately trained about options for homeowners undergoing such relocations and take steps to ensure that information on relevant assistance programs is accurate and readily understandable. Similarly, in June 2012, FHFA announced that Fannie Mae and Freddie Mac will consider a servicemember's receipt of permanent change-of-station orders as making such borrowers eligible for a short-sale, even if the borrower is current on his or her mortgage.

[42]All estimates from our workpaper review are subject to sampling error. For this estimate, we are 95 percent confident that the actual population value is between 45 percent and 52 percent.

included the need to follow up on previous violations and deficiencies, changes in regulatory requirements, and identification of SCRA loans being serviced. To determine the extent to which SCRA compliance was included in examinations of depository institutions and the procedures examiners used to assess SCRA compliance, we reviewed workpapers for examinations conducted by FDIC, Federal Reserve, NCUA, and OCC. We reviewed the workpapers for examinations from 2007 to 2011 for a sample of 152 institutions that service mortgages they hold in their loan portfolios or service mortgages for other institutions.[43] The 152 institutions represented a stratified random sample of institutions based on size and regulator examined from 2007 through 2011. Because officials from some regulators told us that they may not conduct an examination for every institution every 12 months, and because SCRA might not be covered in each risk-based examination, we looked at examinations spanning a 5-year period.

Based on our sample, we found that prudential regulators included a review of SCRA compliance in at least one examination for a greater percentage of large institutions than all other institutions. In this report, the 40 large institutions are comprised of the 10 largest mortgage servicers regulated by each of the four prudential regulators. Specifically, we found that about 70 percent of these large institutions were reviewed for SCRA compliance at least once from 2007 through 2011 compared with an estimated 48 percent of all other institutions for the same period.[44] Officials from one regulator indicated that one reason for this difference might be that the larger institutions conducted more mortgage lending than smaller institutions; therefore, examiners may be more likely to review SCRA compliance at larger institutions.

We also found that the extent to which examiners reviewed for SCRA compliance varied by year. In 2010, examinations for SCRA compliance

[43]We selected a sample of 160 institutions, but a total of 8 were determined to be out of the scope of our study for various reasons, such as being new institutions that had yet to have been examined. See appendix I for additional information about our sampling methodology.

[44]We reviewed examinations for all 40 of the large institutions, and therefore the percentage presented is the percentage of these 40 large institutions, and is not an estimate. For our estimates of the remaining institutions, we are 95 percent confident that the actual population of these institutions that were examined for SCRA is between 45 percent and 52 percent.

occurred in an estimated 26 percent of all institutions, compared with 2007 when about 4 percent of all institutions were reviewed for SCRA. Figure 2 shows the distribution in the percentage of institutions examined for SCRA compliance for each year from 2007 through 2011. Some of the regulatory officials told us that reasons for the differences by year may include the adoption of SCRA interagency examination procedures in 2009 and increased attention to the impacts of the financial crisis on servicemembers in recent years.

Figure 2: Estimated Percentage of Depository Institutions That Serviced Mortgages That Were Examined for SCRA Compliance by Year, 2007 through 2011

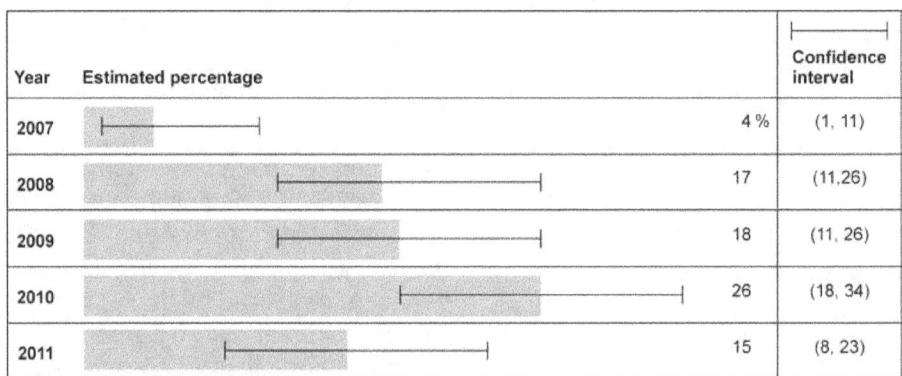

Year	Estimated percentage		Confidence interval
2007		4 %	(1, 11)
2008		17	(11,26)
2009		18	(11, 26)
2010		26	(18, 34)
2011		15	(8, 23)

Source: GAO analysis of prudential regulator examination workpapers.

Note: The percentage of institutions that had an examination in each year is not mutually exclusive. This means that one institution could have had an examination that addressed SCRA in more than 1 year. The error bars represent 95 percent confidence intervals for each of these estimates. The confidence intervals represent the upper and lower bounds of our estimates.

We also found that among just the 40 large institutions, a greater percentage had an SCRA compliance review in 2010 and 2011 compared with earlier years:

- in 2010 and also in 2011, about 40 percent of the institutions had an SCRA review,

- about 13 percent of these institutions were reviewed for SCRA compliance in 2009,

- about 23 percent of these institutions were reviewed for SCRA compliance in 2008, and

- in 2007, 10 percent were reviewed for SCRA compliance.[45]

Our analysis also revealed differences by regulator in the extent to which SCRA was reviewed for compliance. Figure 3 shows that both FDIC and Federal Reserve reviewed a significantly higher percentage of institutions for SCRA compliance compared with NCUA and OCC. It also shows that OCC reviewed a greater percentage of institutions than NCUA. NCUA officials explained that the agency does not have a separate consumer compliance examination function and that consumer compliance is part of its overall evaluation of the safety and soundness of institutions. The officials said that given the recent economic crisis, the agency has placed more focus on the safety and soundness of credit unions than on compliance with consumer regulations. They said that this is part of the reason the percentage of credit unions that received an SCRA compliance review is so low. However, our prior work has found that mortgage servicing problems, including inadequate controls over foreclosure processes, have led to risks to the safety and soundness of depository institutions.[46]

---

[45]We reviewed examinations for all 40 of the large institutions, and therefore the percentages presented are the percentages of these 40 large institutions, and are not estimates.

[46]GAO-11-433, pp. 48-52.

Figure 3: Estimated Percentage of Depository Institutions That Serviced Mortgages That Were Examined for SCRA Compliance by Regulator, 2007 through 2011

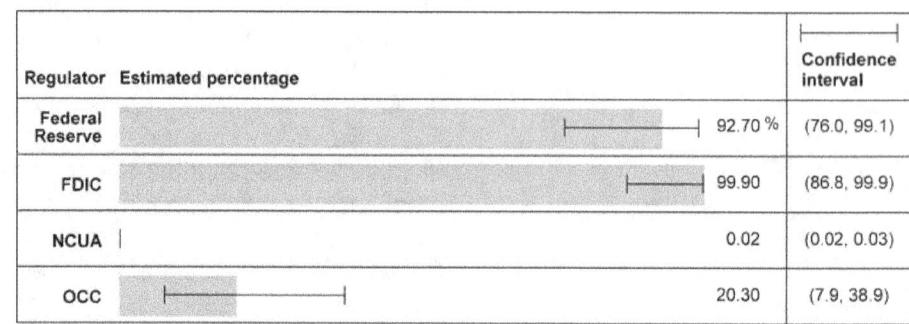

Regulator	Estimated percentage		Confidence interval
Federal Reserve		92.70 %	(76.0, 99.1)
FDIC		99.90	(86.8, 99.9)
NCUA		0.02	(0.02, 0.03)
OCC		20.30	(7.9, 38.9)

Source: GAO analysis of prudential regulator examination workpapers.

Note: Error bars in this graph represent the 95 percent confidence intervals for estimates displayed. Six of the depository institutions in the sample were regulated by the Office of Thrift Supervision (OTS) until July 2011. The Dodd-Frank Act eliminated OTS and supervisory authority of these six depository institutions was transferred to OCC. We included these six institutions in our sample strata for large and OCC-regulated institutions because at the time we selected our sample, these six institutions were under OCC's supervisory authority. OCC officials explained that OTS conducted most of the examinations of these institutions during the period we reviewed and that OTS's examination practices related to SCRA may have differed from those of OCC.

For the estimated 52 percent of institutions that were not examined for SCRA compliance from 2007 through 2011, examiners did not document their reasons for excluding SCRA for at least 95 percent of these institutions.[47] In our review, we found four examinations for which examiners had documented in the workpapers a reason for not including SCRA compliance. For three of these examinations, the reason cited was that examiners had recently examined for SCRA compliance and found no violations, deficiencies, or other concerns. The fourth examination reviewed the depository institutions' progress in addressing consumer compliance issues identified in the previous examination and because SCRA compliance was not one of the issues of concern identified in the previous examination, it was excluded from the examination we reviewed.

Regulatory officials offered a few reasons to explain why an examiner may not include SCRA compliance in an examination. For example, officials from one regulator said that some depository institutions might

---

[47]We are 95 percent confident that the actual population value for institutions that were not examined for SCRA is between 48 percent and 56 percent. We are 95 percent confident that the actual population value for institutions for which examiners failed to document their reasons for excluding SCRA is between 95 percent and 100 percent.

not serve large military populations. Therefore, examiners might not consider compliance with SCRA mortgage protections a substantial risk to these institutions. Additionally, officials from one prudential regulator indicated that examiners may choose to exclude SCRA compliance from an examination if the institution had received few complaints concerning SCRA-related issues. The regulators indicated that they had received very few SCRA complaints related to residential mortgages between 2007 and 2011 compared with the number of consumer complaints they received overall during this period.[48]

Examiners Generally Used Limited Loan Testing

As part of our review of examination workpapers for the 152 institutions in our sample, we collected information on the procedures examiners used to assess compliance with SCRA if an examination reviewed residential mortgage loans or if the workpapers did not specify the loan product being addressed. We included examinations in which the loan product was not specified to help ensure that we reviewed any examination procedures that may have addressed residential mortgages. Our review found a total of 83 institutions for which examiners either reviewed SCRA compliance for residential mortgage loans or did not specify the loan product being reviewed. The figures presented for this analysis are not generalizable to the population of institutions that service mortgages. After reviewing examination guidance and auditing standards, we grouped examiners' documented examination procedures into three categories based on our professional judgment as to the extent that each type of procedure would provide assurance that financial institutions were complying with SCRA:

- *Interviews with depository institution personnel.* This category includes activities in which examiners interviewed staff at the depository institution for information on, among other things, their compliance management systems and whether the institution services loans to servicemembers eligible for SCRA protections.

- *Assessments of depository institutions' compliance management systems.* This category includes instances in which examiners

---

[48]In addition, our review of the regulators' 2007 through 2011 complaint data revealed that collectively they had received 201 SCRA complaints from 2007 through 2011, 88 (44 percent) of which pertained to residential mortgages. This number represents less than 1 percent of all complaints the prudential regulators received during this period.

documented that they reviewed the quality of depository institutions' compliance management systems, such as reviewing institutions' SCRA policies and procedures, internal controls, and training programs.

- *Testing loan files for SCRA compliance.* This category includes activities such as testing a limited number of loan files the institution identified as SCRA-eligible or conducting more comprehensive testing, such as reviewing a statistical sample of loan files.

Of these categories, the first category—interviews with depository institution personnel—provides the least assurance of SCRA compliance because the examiner would be relying primarily on assertions provided by institution personnel rather than an independent assessment or verification of these assertions. The second category—assessments of institutions' compliance management systems—provides greater assurance of SCRA compliance because these procedures require examiners to independently assess the quality of the depository institutions' procedures and internal controls. The final category—testing of loan files—provides even greater assurance of SCRA compliance because examiners can independently verify whether the institution's personnel provided all necessary SCRA protections.

Although in many examinations examiners documented that they used an assortment of examination procedures from different categories to assess compliance with SCRA, we categorized each of the 83 institutions whose SCRA compliance was assessed during the 5-year period of our review by the highest assurance level of the examination procedures that were used in any of the examinations done of that institution from 2007 through 2011. Based on this analysis, we found that only about half of these institutions had any testing conducted during this 5-year period. Specifically, of these 83 institutions, we found that

- 6 institutions had examinations during this period that relied on interviews of depository institution staff to assess SCRA compliance as their highest category of examination procedure,

- 36 institutions had examinations in which the highest category of examination procedure used to assess SCRA compliance was to review the institution's compliance management system, and

- 41 institutions had examinations that involved testing of loan files as the highest category of examination procedure—the examination procedure category that provides a greater level of assurance for SCRA compliance than the previous two categories.

However, at the 41 institutions at which examiners tested loan files, we found that the type of testing conducted was limited. Examiners can choose from different types of testing methods that provide differing levels of assurance that an institution is complying with SCRA. For example, within the testing category, testing a limited sample of loan files that depository institutions identified as SCRA-eligible provides less assurance of compliance because it relies on assertions by depository institutions of SCRA eligibility, whereas testing a statistical sample of loans provides greater assurance because it allows examiners to independently select files for testing, and the results would be representative of the institution's compliance. In the examinations we reviewed, the examiners mostly tested a limited sample of loans that the depository institution had identified as SCRA-eligible and, therefore, provided less assurance that the institution was complying with SCRA. We found no instances between 2007 and 2011 in which examiners tested a statistical sample of either loans in foreclosure or mortgage loan files in general, which would have provided the greatest assurance of an institution's SCRA compliance. By testing only foreclosure files or mortgage loan files that the depository institution had identified as SCRA-eligible, examiners cannot fully determine if the institution has appropriately identified all eligible servicemembers. By expanding the scope of testing to include a larger sample of foreclosure and mortgage loan files, beyond just those files that the depository institution had identified as SCRA-eligible, examiners could better ensure that institutions are appropriately identifying eligible servicemembers and providing them all of the protections to which they are entitled. To minimize the burden on institutions and examiners, such reviews could be conducted as part of samples of loans drawn for examining compliance with other regulatory requirements.

Coordination of SCRA Oversight Lacking

In addition to the prudential regulators, other federal agencies conduct oversight of SCRA compliance. SCRA authorizes DOJ to commence a civil action against any person who engages in a pattern or practice of violating the act or if a violation of the act raises an issue of significant public importance.[49] DOJ staff indicated that they consider military attorneys to be the most likely staff to help ensure that a servicemember is afforded their SCRA protections. For cases in which a military attorney is unable to obtain voluntary compliance from a mortgage servicer or other person or entity doing business with a servicemember, DOJ has a system in place to receive referrals for these cases and to open investigations. DOJ officials told us and military attorneys confirmed that, in most cases, military attorneys are able to resolve SCRA matters without referring them to DOJ. DOJ also receives referrals for SCRA investigations from private attorneys and individual servicemembers and their families. When DOJ receives an SCRA referral, officials investigate the matter and determine if a full investigation should be opened.[50] Investigations can result in DOJ filing a civil action against the party in court for alleged SCRA violations, or a resolution with the party may be reached without filing the case in court.

DOJ filed a total of five cases in court from 2007 through 2011 for SCRA violations. Two of these cases—BAC Home Loans Servicing, LP and Saxon Mortgage Services, Inc.—involved SCRA violations regarding servicemembers' mortgages. In May 2011, DOJ took enforcement actions against both mortgage servicers for wrongfully foreclosing upon active duty servicemembers without obtaining court orders. DOJ alleged that both mortgage servicers did not consistently check the military status of borrowers on whom they foreclosed, resulting in 165 improper foreclosures between 2006 and December 2010 (as listed previously in table 1). In its enforcement actions, DOJ required each of these mortgage servicers to pay damages to servicemembers and conduct a variety of remedial actions. For example, BAC Home Loans Servicing agreed to pay at least $20 million to resolve the lawsuit, and Saxon Mortgage Services agreed to pay at least $2.35 million. The mortgage servicers were also required to, among other things, (1) implement revised SCRA policies and procedures for using the DMDC website, (2) implement a foreclosure monitoring program, (3) provide SCRA compliance training to all applicable employees, and (4) conduct reviews to identify additional

---

[49]50 U.S.C. app. § 597. This provision was added to SCRA in October 2010. *See* Pub. L. 111-275, § 303(a), 124 Stat. 2877.

[50]We use the term investigation to refer to a written or oral inquiry for which a DOJ official spends at least 2 hours investigating. DOJ uses the term matter to describe these instances.

servicemembers who may have had their SCRA rights violated and compensate them. Appendix II discusses these reviews in more detail. In addition to the 5 SCRA cases DOJ filed in court, DOJ opened 45 additional SCRA investigations from referrals it received between 2007 and 2011, 9 of which involved servicemembers' mortgages.[51] One of these referrals involved a servicemember's request to waive the prepayment penalty on her mortgage when she received a permanent change-of-station order and sold her home to move closer to the new base. DOJ was able to reach a resolution with the mortgage servicer without trying the case in court. Another investigation involved allegations of a mortgage servicer charging interest in excess of the SCRA maximum of 6 percent. DOJ officials stated that this investigation was resolved in favor of the servicemember. Finally, in February 2012, DOJ settled with five of the nation's largest mortgage servicers for a variety of improper mortgage servicing procedures, including allegations of SCRA violations. More information on the National Mortgage Settlement is contained in appendix II.

Other federal agencies that operate mortgage programs also oversee certain aspects of SCRA compliance. For example, to participate in FHA's mortgage programs, mortgage servicers must comply with the agency's program requirements, which include complying with all applicable laws and regulations, including SCRA. FHA officials explained that they use a risk-based approach to monitor the institutions that service the loans the agency insures. Officials told us that from 2007 through 2011, FHA conducted about 200 mortgage servicer monitoring reviews. They explained that each review consists of a sample of the mortgage servicer's loan files and FHA staff use a checklist to help ensure that the mortgage servicer is in compliance with a variety of servicing requirements for each loan in the sample. One of the requirements reviewed for each loan is the distribution of the HUD counseling notice that includes information on SCRA eligibility to borrowers who are at least 45 days delinquent. Agency officials explained that a more thorough review of SCRA compliance is conducted if a mortgage servicer has identified that the borrower is an active duty servicemember. For loans that a mortgage servicer has marked with a code to indicate that the borrower is an active duty servicemember, FHA staff conduct additional

---

[51]Because DOJ does not document inquiries that require less than 2 hours of investigation, the number of investigations listed here may underestimate the number of SCRA referrals DOJ received.

steps to better ensure that the mortgage servicer has provided the servicemember appropriate SCRA protections, as well as additional protections that FHA provides to active duty servicemembers who have FHA-insured loans. These steps include ensuring that the interest rate has been appropriately adjusted and that foreclosure was postponed. FHA officials stated that they rely on mortgage servicers to appropriately identify active duty servicemembers. Although they may review SCRA compliance on specific loans, FHA officials told us that their reviews are not intended to assess the adequacy of the mortgage servicers' SCRA compliance policies and procedures or to determine whether these policies are functioning for all of a servicer's activities. As a result of FHA's servicer monitoring reviews, some SCRA compliance problems have been identified. For example, FHA officials told us that between 2007 and 2011 the agency found two instances of SCRA noncompliance during its mortgage servicer monitoring reviews. One of these instances involved a mortgage servicer failing to send the HUD counseling notice that includes information on SCRA eligibility to borrowers delinquent 45 or more days, and the other violation involved a mortgage servicer failing to verify a borrower's active duty status prior to foreclosure.

Although VA interacts with mortgage servicers as part of its Home Loan Guaranty Program, VA officials explained that the program currently does not conduct in-depth reviews of mortgage servicers' policies and procedures and loan files to review overall compliance with SCRA mortgage protections. The officials explained that they are in the process of finalizing a program that will conduct on-site audits of mortgage servicers' functions and that they expect the program to be implemented in late 2012. VA officials explained that this program will include reviews of servicers' loan files and policies and procedures for monitoring and identifying SCRA-eligible borrowers to determine servicers' overall compliance with SCRA mortgage protections. Officials explained that in the wake of recently identified SCRA violations, they conducted a review of all VA loan files that were in foreclosure from October 2009 to January 2011 to determine if any of the borrowers were possibly eligible for SCRA mortgage protections. The officials said that they identified approximately 30,000 borrowers in foreclosure during that period and that they conducted an in-depth review of 47 loans that were potentially eligible for SCRA mortgage protections. VA determined that none of these borrowers were improperly foreclosed upon. They have recently expanded this review to include a longer time period, but as of June 2012, they had not completed the review to determine if any borrowers were improperly foreclosed upon.

VA officials explained that they do conduct reviews of the adequacy of servicing being conducted by servicers. These reviews—Adequacy of Servicing reviews—are conducted on all loans over 120 days delinquent to determine if servicers have provided adequate servicing to borrowers, but according to VA officials, they are intended to explore loss mitigation options and not to examine for SCRA compliance. The officials explained that during these reviews, VA reviews mortgage servicers' notes on the account to determine if they have provided adequate servicing to the borrower. Specifically, they check to see if the mortgage servicer has contacted the borrower, if a reason for default has been determined, if loss mitigation options have been considered, and why any loss mitigation options that were considered were not completed. Officials explained that if the mortgage servicer has taken the appropriate steps, VA would determine that the servicing provided was adequate. If VA determines that the servicing being provided was not adequate, or if the servicer was unable to contact the borrower, it conducts supplemental servicing on the loan and works with the borrower directly to explore loss mitigation options. According to VA officials, they may learn during these reviews that the loan involves an active duty servicemember. However, the Adequacy of Servicing reviews currently do not evaluate the extent to which servicers have assessed whether borrowers are eligible for SCRA mortgage protections. They also explained that while their procedures for conducting these reviews do not address reviewing for compliance with SCRA mortgage protections, VA loan technicians encourage borrowers to review their SCRA mortgage protections with military attorneys. Additionally, VA officials explained that they do not have a mechanism for tracking if these reviews have identified SCRA-eligible borrowers. As part of VA's mission to serve servicemembers, VA officials told us that they try to ensure that servicemembers have received every opportunity to keep their homes and avoid foreclosure. VA officials explained that they rely on federal regulators to investigate and enforce statutory requirements, such as SCRA. However, given that VA staff also oversee servicers' activities, they do have the opportunity to review servicers' efforts to determine SCRA eligibility, such as by making an inquiry with the servicer of the loan or consulting DOD records to determine if the borrower is an active duty servicemember. Without such a review, the extent to which the agency is ensuring servicemembers are receiving all protections to which they are entitled is not clear.

The enterprises—Fannie Mae and Freddie Mac—also conduct SCRA compliance monitoring at the mortgage servicers that service loans on their behalf. This monitoring focuses on enforcing contractual requirements between the enterprises and mortgage servicers to ensure that mortgage servicers are following the servicing guidelines issued by the enterprises. The servicing guidelines outline mortgage servicers' compliance obligations for several different laws and regulations, including SCRA. The SCRA components of the guidelines include information for mortgage servicers on, among other things, how SCRA relief is initiated and how interest rates are reduced, as well as foreclosure proceedings and credit reporting. Enterprise officials explained that SCRA compliance is not included in each review conducted. If it is included, Fannie Mae officials explained that examiners seek to understand how a mortgage servicer checks for SCRA compliance and conducts testing of the servicers accounting methods for SCRA compliance.[52] For example, if a servicemember has an interest rate that is greater than 6 percent, examiners test to ensure that interest rate and payment amounts have been properly reduced. Freddie Mac officials told us they assess the mortgage servicer's understanding of SCRA and the procedures in place to ensure compliance. The enterprises' SCRA compliance monitoring efforts have identified some instances of noncompliance. For example, Fannie Mae identified 13 instances of noncompliance with its SCRA guidelines between 2007 and 2011, and Freddie Mac has identified 2 instances. These instances of noncompliance involved issues such as mortgage servicers not having comprehensive SCRA compliance policies and procedures and mortgage servicers not properly verifying the active duty status of servicemembers. Officials from FHFA—the enterprises' regulator—stated that its supervisory focus for SCRA compliance is to confirm that the enterprises are taking steps to ensure that the mortgage servicers with which they have contracts comply with the contracts' requirements which include compliance with applicable laws.

Although the prudential regulators, FHA, VA, and FHFA all have a role in helping ensure that mortgage servicers provide appropriate SCRA protections to eligible servicemembers, currently none of these entities

---

[52]A Fannie Mae official told us that as of November 2011, the examiner guidance they used for SCRA compliance reviews only included procedures for examining for compliance with the interest rate provisions of SCRA, but that they were working to update it for 2012 to incorporate compliance with SCRA's foreclosure provisions.

share information related to SCRA compliance with one another.[53] While the extent of oversight conducted by these entities varies, they do review for some of the same SCRA provisions, such as those related to interest rate reductions and foreclosures. Furthermore, some of the mortgage servicers that participate in FHA's and VA's loan programs and service loans on behalf of the enterprises are also subject to oversight by one of the prudential regulators, which review for SCRA compliance during their examinations. Although these agencies obtain SCRA-related information about many of the same institutions, FHA, VA, and FHFA officials stated that they have not coordinated with the prudential regulators on SCRA compliance issues. Further, FHFA officials stated that while they participate in some forums with the prudential regulators to coordinate on various issues, they were not aware of any coordination related to SCRA compliance.

In our work on the many agencies that are involved in the federal financial regulatory system, we have previously stated that collaboration among financial regulatory agencies with common responsibilities is essential to ensuring consistent and effective supervisory practices.[54] Further, we have previously reported that federal agencies and prudential regulators do coordinate on oversight of other consumer protection laws, such as the Fair Housing Act and Equal Credit Opportunity Act, known collectively as "fair lending laws."[55] Similar to oversight of SCRA, responsibility for oversight of the fair lending laws is shared among the prudential regulators and other federal agencies, including DOJ, HUD, and the Federal Trade Commission. We reported that these agencies had taken several steps to establish common policies and procedures and share

---

[53]The prudential regulators already have an agreement to share such information with another financial regulator. In May 2012, the prudential regulators and the Consumer Financial Protection Bureau issued a Memorandum of Understanding (MOU) that clarifies how the agencies will coordinate their supervisory activities. Under the MOU, the agencies will coordinate examinations and other supervisory activities and share certain material supervisory information concerning compliance with federal consumer financial laws and certain other federal laws that regulate consumer financial products and services, including SCRA.

[54]GAO, *Financial Market Regulation: Agencies Engaged in Consolidated Supervision Can Strengthen Performance Measurement and Collaboration*, GAO-07-154 (Washington, D.C.: Mar. 15, 2007).

[55]GAO, *Fair Lending: Data Limitations and the Fragmented U.S. Financial Regulatory Structure Challenge Federal Oversight and Enforcement Efforts*, GAO-09-704 (Washington, D.C.: July 15, 2009).

information about their fair lending oversight programs. For example, the agencies established the Interagency Fair Lending Task Force to develop a coordinated approach to address discrimination in lending and adopted a policy statement on how the various agencies were to conduct oversight and enforce the fair lending laws. At that time, federal officials said that coordinating on fair lending issues allows the agencies to exchange information on a range of common issues, informally discuss fair lending policy, and confer about current trends or challenges in fair lending oversight and enforcement. FHFA officials explained that the agency has existing memorandums of understanding with prudential regulators and HUD that establish the protocols they use to discuss trends, risks, and other emerging issues on a variety of topics with these other agencies, but that SCRA has not been a topic during these discussions. FHFA does not currently have a memorandum of understanding with VA to share information, but the officials explained that they have worked with the agency in the past on issues such as appraisals and that they have done so through letter arrangements that allow them to share information. These existing arrangements could provide a mechanism for SCRA information to be shared between FHFA and the prudential regulators, FHA, and VA. However, currently no such sharing arrangements exist between the prudential regulators, FHA, and VA. Although FHA, VA, and the enterprises that FHFA oversees have identified limited instances of SCRA violations in recent years, the sharing of information related to SCRA trends, emerging risks, or types of weaknesses found in mortgage servicers' policies among all agencies that play a role in SCRA compliance oversight could increase awareness of potential problems and improve their ability to identify SCRA violations.

Challenges in Ensuring Servicemembers' Awareness of SCRA Protections

DOD and DHS Education Efforts

Under SCRA, DOD services' Secretaries and the Secretary of Homeland Security have the primary responsibility for ensuring that servicemembers receive information on their SCRA rights and protections.[56] Servicemembers are informed of their SCRA rights in a variety of ways. For example, briefings are provided on military bases and during deployment activities; legal assistance attorneys provide counseling; and a number of outreach media, such as publications and websites, are aimed at informing servicemembers of their SCRA rights. According to DOD officials, the legal assistance attorneys are primarily responsible for leading the military's SCRA education efforts. Each of the military services, including the Coast Guard under DHS, operates a number of legal assistance offices throughout the country.[57] Legal assistance offices are operated by military and civilian legal assistance attorneys who are responsible for providing support to servicemembers on a variety of legal issues, including family law and estate planning.[58] As part of their responsibilities, they inform servicemembers about their rights and benefits under SCRA.

Legal assistance attorneys provide SCRA support to servicemembers using various methods. We spoke with legal assistance attorneys at six military installations across the five services. They told us that they

---

[56]Section 105, Codified at 50 U.S.C. App §515 and §690 of the National Defense Authorization Act of Fiscal Year 2006, P.L. 109-113, codified at 50 U.S.C. App §515a.

[57]As of May 2012, there were a total of 175 legal assistance offices throughout the country and over 60 legal assistance offices located internationally.

[58]10 U.S.C 1044. All regular, active duty servicemembers and members of the reserve components on active duty for 30 days or more are eligible to obtain legal support from a legal assistance office. For members of the reserve components, this access extends for a period twice the length of the servicemembers' active duty period when the servicemember is no longer on active duty service.

provide servicemembers with information on SCRA during routine briefings on military installations, in handouts, and during one-on-one sessions with individual servicemembers. Two legal assistance attorneys told us that they alert installation staff, including unit commanders, to direct servicemembers to their legal assistance offices if they have a problem. Legal assistance attorneys also told us that they will contact depository institutions on behalf of servicemembers to help them receive their SCRA protections. Some legal assistance attorneys also told us that they provide templates of letters for servicemembers to send to their mortgage servicer to request a reduction in their mortgage interest rate. Additionally, legal assistance attorneys told us that they will refer servicemembers to the American Bar Association's (ABA) Military Pro Bono Project if they are unable to resolve an SCRA matter for a servicemember. ABA's program connects active duty servicemembers to pro bono attorneys who assist them with civil legal problems.[59]

SCRA requires that servicemembers be informed of the rights and protections available under SCRA upon entry into the military, during initial orientation training, and, in the cases of members of the reserve components, when called to active duty for a period of more than 1 year.[60] Predeployment briefings generally occur at the military installation that deploys the servicemember and, in addition to SCRA, cover a range of other legal and financial issues, such as the preparation of wills and powers of attorney. According to DOD officials, members of the reserve components may receive this briefing numerous times at their home station prior to deployment. Servicemembers are also provided with an additional opportunity to learn about their rights under SCRA upon returning from deployment. According to DOD officials, because some SCRA protections extend for a 9- or 12-month period beyond servicemembers' active duty service, obtaining information at the end of deployment is critical for those servicemembers who will no longer be on active duty and will lose access to military-provided legal assistance. As a result, the Army reserve component—which includes the Army Reserve and Army National Guard and is the largest portion of the reserve

---

[59]Only junior-enlisted (E6 or below) servicemembers are eligible for assistance through the Military Pro Bono Project unless there are compelling circumstances and at the discretion of the pro bono attorney or firm.

[60]Section 105, Codified at 50 U.S.C. App §515 and §690 of the National Defense Authorization Act of Fiscal Year 2006, P.L. 109-113, codified at 50 U.S.C. App §515a.

components—requires that members receive standardized post-deployment training on SCRA.

DOD and DHS use a number of other methods to deliver SCRA information to servicemembers, including military training courses, publications, websites, and other family support services. For example, DHS officials told us that all Coast Guard members are informed of their SCRA rights during basic training. Some others may receive additional SCRA training during their initial officer training at the Coast Guard Academy or other advanced classes. DOD also publishes general articles in newsletters and installation publications explaining servicemembers' SCRA rights and more specific articles on the relationship between mortgage difficulties and SCRA. Additionally, several military websites contain information on SCRA, including websites for individual services and military installations and sites such as Military OneSource—a DOD online resource that is staffed with counselors who offer assistance to servicemembers on a variety of topics, including financial counseling.[61] DOD also provides financial management and family support services through the family readiness centers located at military installations. These centers provide general financial management counseling on topics such as reducing debt and saving for college to servicemembers' families during periods of deployment and also share information on SCRA and refer family members to the legal assistance office if they have an SCRA issue.

Other SCRA Outreach Efforts

Other federal agencies also provide SCRA outreach and support to servicemembers and financial institutions in a variety of ways, including oral briefings, written notifications, and websites. For example, VA officials told us that some servicemembers who leave active duty service participate in a multiday briefing conducted in partnership with VA, DOD, and the Department of Labor. This briefing discusses reentering civilian life, SCRA protections, and veterans' benefits. Additionally, both VA and FHA provide SCRA-related outreach to the institutions that participate in their mortgage programs. For example, VA periodically sends written notifications to all of its loan servicers reminding them of their compliance responsibilities and alerts them to changes in the act when they occur. FHA also provides information to its mortgage servicers on SCRA. Its

---

[61]See www.militaryonesource.mil.

website contains a list of questions and answers for mortgage servicers on SCRA, servicemembers' eligibility criteria, and FHA policies with respect to servicing FHA-insured mortgages in compliance with SCRA.

The Consumer Financial Protection Bureau (CFPB) has an Office of Servicemember Affairs that also plays a role in providing SCRA outreach to servicemembers and mortgage servicers responsible for complying with the act. As of May 30, 2012, CFPB officials had conducted 37 visits to military installations and National Guard units and met with legal assistance attorneys to discuss consumer protection issues servicemembers have been facing, including SCRA. CFPB also sent letters to 25 large mortgage servicers in 2011 alerting them of servicemembers' rights under SCRA and their responsibilities to comply with the act. The letters specifically urged mortgage servicers to educate their employees about SCRA and review their loan files to ensure compliance with the law. Additionally, CFPB has held meetings in which representatives from DOD and DHS and other federal agencies, financial institutions, and trade associations discussed issues related to SCRA compliance. CFPB officials also held a forum in which financial institutions discussed activities—some that go beyond those required by SCRA— they were undertaking to assist servicemembers' with their mortgages. In July 2011, CFPB and the Judge Advocate Generals of the Army, Marine Corps, Navy, Air Force, and Coast Guard developed a joint statement of principles to provide stronger protections for servicemembers in connection with consumer financial products and services. Finally, through its consumer response function, CFPB also works directly with servicemembers by collecting consumer complaints against depository institutions and coordinating those complaints with servicemembers' depository institutions and if necessary, the appropriate legal assistance offices.

Finally, military servicemember groups also assist servicemembers with SCRA issues. Organizations such as the National Military Family Association, the Military Officers Association of America, the Reserve Officers Association, and others provide information on SCRA to their members in a variety of ways. A representative from one military servicemember group explained that its website—which contains background information on SCRA and legal reviews of specific SCRA provisions—is the group's primary means of providing information to servicemembers and the public on SCRA issues. Other representatives with whom we spoke said that they provide information to their members when changes to SCRA have occurred. For example, one military servicemember group highlights applicable legislative changes in weekly electronic notifications to its members.

Servicemembers Face Challenges Asserting Their SCRA Protections, Raising Questions about Training Effectiveness

DOD officials, legal assistance attorneys, and representatives of military servicemember groups with whom we spoke noted a number of challenges with ensuring that servicemembers are aware of their SCRA protections. One main challenge cited was servicemembers' retention of the SCRA information they receive from DOD and DHS. Attorneys at each of the six legal assistance offices told us that servicemembers are not aware of the full extent of their SCRA rights. In addition, several military servicemember group representatives, a National Guard Bureau official, and an SCRA expert told us that despite available information on SCRA, servicemembers are not adequately prepared to invoke their rights when needed.

According to DOD officials, the bulk of the SCRA education provided to servicemembers occurs at military installations that focus on regular active duty servicemembers. However, members of the reserve components—those most likely to qualify for SCRA's mortgage protections—may not be located at military installations and, therefore, have less access to these services and trainings. One DOD official told us that members of the reserve components may receive SCRA briefings at their home station. However, legal assistance attorneys at five of the six legal assistance offices with whom we spoke told us that members of the reserve components have limited access to legal assistance offices on military installations when they are not on active duty. Having this limited access to legal assistance could affect reserve components members' ability to avail themselves of their SCRA protections when needed. Additionally, some members of the reserve components face geographic challenges with accessing legal assistance offices due to their distance from military installations. About half of the military installations in the United States are located in just 10 states, while members of the reserve components live throughout the country. For example, the Chief Legal Assistant for the Ninth Coast Guard District explained that the legal assistance office for that district is located in Cleveland, Ohio, but the office provides legal services to the entire Great Lakes Region.

Another challenge in ensuring that servicemembers are aware of their SCRA protections when needed is the effectiveness of the educational briefings provided by DOD and DHS. As discussed above, SCRA requires that servicemembers receive SCRA training upon entry into the military, during initial orientation training, and, for members of the reserve components, when called to active duty for a period of more than 1 year. However, legal assistance attorneys who conduct this training and military servicemember groups explained that its effectiveness is diminished because of the volume of information presented, the timing of the training, and the availability of legal assistance resources. For example, four military officials told us that during predeployment activities and annual National Guard weekend training activities, servicemembers attend multiple, back-to-back briefings, which cover a variety of legal and financial issues that are focused on a number of important topics, such as family law and estate planning. One military attorney referred to these briefings as "baptism by a fire hose" when trying to illustrate the volume of information provided to servicemembers at these critical times. Further, military attorneys with whom we spoke told us that the amount of time legal assistance attorneys are able to spend with servicemembers during pre- and postdeployment activities is limited due to the volume of servicemembers deploying and returning from deployment. For example, one military attorney told us that legal assistance attorneys might assist 250 deploying servicemembers with their legal affairs prior to deployment and that during deployment there is limited time available to provide legal assistance. Another legal assistance attorney stated that it would be beneficial for members of the reserve components to have more time to access military legal assistance resources when they return from deployment because of concerns that they do not retain the information they receive during postdeployment briefings. One legal assistance attorney that assists members of the reserves specifically explained that when he provides SCRA-related briefings to deployed servicemembers who should have received SCRA briefings prior to deployment; many seem like they are hearing the information for the first time. He suggested that servicemembers' retention of information could be improved if deploying servicemembers receive more comprehensive briefings with smaller groups of servicemembers. Additionally, a National Guard Bureau official told us that predeployment briefings contain too much information for servicemembers to absorb, including the relatively small portions of the briefings that include information on SCRA. These methods of providing SCRA information to servicemembers raise concerns about their ability to retain the information they receive during these trainings.

Without adequate awareness, servicemembers may not take full advantage of their protections under SCRA. As discussed above, the methods of SCRA training and outreach provided by DOD and DHS to regular active duty servicemembers and members of the reserve components may not be adequate to ensure that these servicemembers are aware of and benefiting from the full protections provided by the act.

In 2008, DOD asked in its annual Status of Forces Surveys if active duty servicemembers and members of the reserve components had received SCRA trainings. Forty-seven percent of members of the reserve components—including those who had been activated in 2008—reported in the survey that they had received SCRA training and only 35 percent of regular active duty servicemembers reported that they had received training.[62] While these numbers may not reflect the number of servicemembers who received SCRA training, they do provide an indication as to the number of servicemembers who recalled receiving such training. DOD also surveys servicemembers on a variety of issues related to their benefits; however, according to DOD officials who conduct these surveys, servicemembers have not been surveyed on the effectiveness of DOD's SCRA educational efforts. DHS officials also told us they have not evaluated the effectiveness of their SCRA education methods to members of the Coast Guard and Coast Guard Reserve. In addition to surveying servicemembers on the effectiveness of SCRA-related education methods, DOD and DHS could use other techniques to assess the effectiveness of their education efforts. For example, servicemembers could be tested after a period of time to determine how much information they retained from the SCRA component of their predeployment briefings. Additionally, focus groups could be held with servicemembers to review the understandability of written materials provided on SCRA. Without understanding the extent to which existing SCRA educational efforts are effective, DOD and DHS are not able to determine if their methods are adequate to ensure that servicemembers avail themselves of the benefits to which they are entitled.

Conclusions

Ensuring that mortgage servicers fully comply with SCRA can protect servicemembers from undue financial harm. Our analysis of risk-based compliance examinations conducted by the four prudential regulators estimated that about half of all the depository institutions that serviced mortgages were reviewed for SCRA compliance from 2007 through 2011. However, during these examinations, examiners only conducted testing of loan files at 41 of the 83 institutions for which we reviewed the procedures

---

[62]DOD *Status of Forces Survey of Active Duty Members* (August 2008) and *Status of Forces Survey of Reserve Component Members* (November 2008). The margin of error for both active duty servicemembers and reserve components members is plus or minus 2 percent. Survey results do not include responses from members of the Coast Guard and Coast Guard Reserve.

used by examiners over the 5-year period to verify that mortgage servicers' SCRA compliance processes and controls were functioning properly. For these 41 institutions, examiners did not use the testing procedures most likely to detect instances of noncompliance. Examination guidance and auditing standards suggest that testing is a part of effective monitoring. Furthermore, additional testing of loan files using methods that provide greater assurance of compliance is warranted given that thousands of violations at some large mortgage servicers have been documented through federal agencies' targeted reviews and mortgage servicers' own internal reviews, but not through the prudential regulators' routine compliance examinations. Without additional testing of foreclosure files and, as appropriate, other mortgage loan files not identified by the depository institution as SCRA-eligible, and without employing testing methods that provide greater assurance of compliance, prudential regulators may not be able to determine whether these institutions are extending protections to all eligible servicemembers.

Although not a direct regulator of financial institutions that service mortgages, VA does interact with mortgage servicers as part of its Home Loan Guaranty program and therefore has an interest in ensuring that these institutions are complying with SCRA. However, the current level of monitoring that VA conducts of mortgage servicers that participate in its program provides little assurance that eligible servicemembers with VA-guaranteed loans are receiving their full SCRA mortgage protections. By not routinely reviewing mortgage servicers' overall compliance with SCRA mortgage protections, the agency cannot be assured that mortgage servicers participating in its program have policies and procedures that function properly to provide these protections. The agency's development of a new program to conduct on-site audits of mortgage servicers' overall operations provides a good opportunity for the agency to expand its efforts related to SCRA compliance. Further, if VA determines that servicers' loss mitigation efforts have either not been successful or adequate during its Adequacy of Servicing reviews, it provides supplemental servicing on loans. During its Adequacy of Servicing reviews and while conducting supplemental servicing, VA would have the opportunity to take steps to determine if servicers assessed whether borrowers were eligible for SCRA protections. Because the agency's entire mission is dedicated to benefiting individuals who have served the country through military service, expanding its procedures to review for SCRA compliance at mortgage servicers that participate in its mortgage program could help the agency achieve its mission and better ensure that servicemembers are receiving all benefits to which they are entitled.

Because multiple federal agencies' play a role in ensuring that mortgage servicers provide SCRA protections to eligible servicemembers, sharing information on SCRA compliance could benefit these agencies' respective SCRA oversight efforts. Most agencies responsible for SCRA oversight conduct risk-based reviews and therefore do not always include SCRA compliance in their reviews. Sharing information on SCRA compliance issues could alert agencies to potential problems and improve agencies' ability to identify SCRA violations. We have previously found that collaboration among supervisory agencies can lead to more effective supervision and that such collaboration does occur for certain consumer compliance laws. However, no such sharing of information related to SCRA compliance information currently takes place routinely between the prudential regulators, FHA, VA, and FHFA. Further, because these entities monitor SCRA compliance at many of the same institutions, the sharing of information could help them to more quickly identify compliance problems that may adversely affect servicemembers. Many of these agencies already have existing mechanisms for sharing information that could be used or expanded to periodically share information on SCRA compliance.

The Secretaries of the Army, Navy, Air Force, and Homeland Security are responsible for educating servicemembers on their SCRA rights. DOD and DHS provide this information through a variety of methods throughout servicemembers' military careers. However, servicemembers may often be unaware of their SCRA rights for a variety of reasons, such as the volume and variety of information they must retain from educational briefings. Members of the reserve components in particular face unique challenges that can affect whether they learn of and are able to obtain assistance with SCRA protections because they have more limited access to military legal assistance locations and to SCRA-related training opportunities. Additionally, the recently created CFPB's Office of Servicemember Affairs has been working with DOD and DHS to identify opportunities to increase servicemembers' awareness of SCRA protections and its results could provide useful information to assist in this effort. While DOD has surveyed servicemembers on whether they had received SCRA training, neither DOD nor DHS has assessed the effectiveness of their educational methods to determine if better ways exist to ensure that servicemembers retain the information they receive on SCRA and can recall it when they need it. Without such an assessment, such as by using focus groups of servicemembers or testing to reinforce retention of SCRA information, DOD and DHS may not be able to ensure they are reaching servicemembers in the most effective manner.

Recommendations for Executive Action

To better ensure SCRA compliance oversight, we recommend that the Comptroller of the Currency, the Chairman of the Board of Governors of the Federal Reserve System, the Chairman of the Federal Deposit Insurance Corporation, and Chairman of the National Credit Union Administration take steps to increase the frequency with which examiners (1) conduct testing of foreclosure files and as applicable, other mortgage loan files; and (2) employ testing methods that provide greater assurance that mortgage servicers are complying with SCRA.

To help ensure that VA assists servicemembers with remaining in their homes and avoiding foreclosure, the Secretary of Veterans Affairs should ensure that a review for SCRA compliance is included in the department's new mortgage servicer monitoring program and that additional steps to assess SCRA compliance are taken by VA staff during its Adequacy of Servicing reviews and while conducting supplemental servicing.

Additionally, to increase agencies' awareness of potential problems with SCRA compliance, the Comptroller of the Currency, the Chairman of the Board of Governors of the Federal Reserve System, the Chairman of the Federal Deposit Insurance Corporation, the Chairman of the National Credit Union Administration, the Acting Director of the Federal Housing Finance Agency, the Secretary of Housing and Urban Development, and the Secretary of Veterans Affairs should explore options to use existing mechanisms or develop new ones to share information related to SCRA compliance oversight.

Finally, the Secretary of Defense—through the Secretaries of the Army, Air Force, and Navy—and the Secretary of Homeland Security should assess the effectiveness of their efforts to educate servicemembers on SCRA to determine better ways for making servicemembers aware of their SCRA rights and benefits, including improving the ways in which members of the reserve components obtain such information.

Agency Comments and Our Evaluation

We requested comments on a draft of this report from CFPB, DHS, DOJ, DOD, FDIC, Federal Reserve, FHFA, HUD, NCUA, OCC, and VA. We received formal written comments from DHS, DOD, FDIC, Federal Reserve, FHFA, HUD, NCUA, OCC, and VA; these are presented in appendixes III through XI, respectively. We also received technical comments from CFPB, DOJ, DOD, FDIC, Federal Reserve, FHFA, OCC, and VA, which we incorporated as appropriate.

Federal Reserve, NCUA, and OCC agreed to take actions in response to our recommendations that they increase the frequency with which their examiners conduct testing of mortgage and foreclosure files and employ testing methods that will provide greater assurance of mortgage servicers' compliance with SCRA.

- The Federal Reserve's Director of the Division of Consumer and Community Affairs noted that Federal Reserve examiners apply interagency examination procedures to test the sufficiency of a depository institution's program for ensuring its employees provide appropriate protections to active duty servicemembers, and that it will work with the other federal financial regulators to consider appropriate ways to update the interagency SCRA examination procedures. The Director's letter notes that Federal Reserve considers interviews with bank staff and reviews institutions' compliance management systems to be types of examiner testing. Although our report acknowledges that such steps can provide useful information regarding an institution's SCRA compliance, we recommended that the regulators provide greater assurance of SCRA compliance by increasing the frequency of loan file testing.

- NCUA's Executive Director agreed that additional testing of loan files would provide greater assurance of SCRA compliance. His letter also notes that NCUA has made recent changes to its examination process to raise the importance of consumer protection issues, noting that beginning with its 2011 examinations, staff separate from safety and soundness examiners review the lending practices of federal credit unions to ensure compliance with SCRA. Further, NCUA noted that it has also incorporated reviews for SCRA compliance into its analysis and investigations of complaints.

- The Comptroller of the Currency noted that OCC will update its examination guidelines to ensure that a review of SCRA compliance is conducted during each supervisory cycle for its regulated institutions, and that such reviews will include the testing of loan files selected using an appropriate methodology to assess compliance with SCRA.

FDIC's Director of their Division of Depositor and Consumer Protection did not comment on our recommendation but agreed that testing a representative sample of loans for compliance with SCRA is an effective tool to assess compliance with SCRA for large mortgage servicers. However, his letter also noted that having examiners interview bank employees also serves as an effective tool for assessing compliance with consumer protection laws and regulations, and that such interviews are often used to verify that the depository institution is conducting sufficient employee training and is enforcing its policies and procedures. We agree that conducting interviews of depository institution personnel can be a useful procedure to examine for SCRA compliance, but supplementing such actions with increased testing of loan files provides an even greater level of assurance that an institution is complying with SCRA.

VA concurred with our recommendation that they ensure that a review for SCRA compliance is included in its new mortgage servicer monitoring program and also indicated their staff would be taking additional steps to assess SCRA compliance during Adequacy of Servicing reviews and while conducting supplemental servicing. In a written response, VA's Chief of Staff noted several activities the agency conducts to help ensure that veterans are aware of their SCRA protections. He stated that VA will revalidate and, as necessary, revise its focus and procedures to ensure veteran borrowers are receiving all SCRA protections to which they are entitled. Additionally, he noted that VA will include in its mortgage servicer monitoring program a review to ensure that servicers' appropriately afford SCRA-eligible borrowers their mortgage protections as part of their loss mitigation efforts. Finally, he said that VA will incorporate additional steps into its Adequacy of Servicing reviews to assess whether the servicer appropriately provided SCRA mortgage protections to eligible borrowers.

Federal Reserve, FHFA, HUD, NCUA, OCC, and VA agreed with our recommendation that the federal agencies involved in overseeing mortgage servicers' SCRA compliance should explore using existing mechanisms or developing new ones to share information related to SCRA compliance oversight.

- Federal Reserve Division of Consumer and Community Affairs Director noted that additional interagency collaboration related to SCRA compliance trends and emerging risks may be appropriate and useful in improving supervisory practices related to SCRA compliance, and she agreed to explore other opportunities to share information related to SCRA compliance with other federal agencies. She stated that their staff are currently planning an interagency servicemember financial protection webinar for financial industry participants that is to include panelists from the federal supervisory agencies, as well as representatives from other agencies with SCRA oversight responsibility.

- FHFA's Deputy Director for the Division of Enterprise Regulation also agreed that increased information sharing among supervisors of mortgage lending industry participants could assist in identifying potential compliance problems and in some cases could improve the identification of SCRA violations. He noted that FHFA's supervision function will consider whether the agency's existing memorandums of understanding are sufficient or should be expanded to cover more types of information or more agencies to broaden information sharing on issues of supervisory concern, including SCRA compliance. He also noted that the supervision function would consider whether compliance oversight would be improved by developing processes for more frequent routine communications with supervisors of other market participants subject to mortgage lending compliance requirements.

- HUD's Acting Assistant Secretary for Housing-Federal Housing Commissioner agreed that HUD should participate in agencies' discussions to explore options to share information related to SCRA compliance, noting that HUD's should be a participatory role rather than a leadership one because it does not have responsibility for overseeing SCRA. Her letter also notes they believe that the scope of such collaboration should be broadened beyond just SCRA compliance to include all agencies' mutual interests in single family housing issues, which we agree could be useful.

- The NCUA Executive Director's letter notes that NCUA will use its participation in FFIEC and other interagency working groups to share information regarding the supervision of financial institutions and compliance concerns, and that it currently shares information with CFPB regarding consumer compliance oversight and is working with federal financial regulators to develop tools to facilitate information sharing.

- The Comptroller of the Currency stated in his response that OCC will continue to be an active member of the FFIEC Task Force on Consumer Compliance, which is an interagency organization that works collectively to develop examiner guidance and examination procedures and to discuss emerging risks or trends regarding new products and services. He also noted that OCC, the other prudential regulators, and CFPB have signed a memorandum of understanding on supervisory coordination that outlines the coordination of examinations and the sharing of compliance oversight information, including information on SCRA.

- VA's Chief of Staff noted that VA will collaborate with the agencies involved in SCRA compliance oversight to share information related to SCRA compliance.

FDIC did not comment on this recommendation.

DHS concurred and DOD partially concurred with our recommendation that they assess the effectiveness of their efforts to educate servicemembers on SCRA to determine better ways for making servicemembers aware of their SCRA rights and benefits, including improving the ways in which members of the reserve components obtain such information. DHS's Director of Departmental GAO-OIG Liaison Office noted that the Coast Guard strives to keep all its members fully aware of SCRA benefits and rights and that it will explore measures to assess the effectiveness of these efforts in the future. DOD's Office of Legal Policy Director stated that the education and protection of servicemembers is DOD's highest priority and that it continuously evaluates the effectiveness of training to servicemembers on their protections under SCRA and that it will continue to do so bearing our recommendation in mind. His letter also notes that DOD recently testified before Congress on efforts to conduct a survey on financial issues affecting servicemembers which will further inform DOD's efforts.

We are sending copies of this report to appropriate congressional committees, the Chairman of the Board of Governors of the Federal Reserve System, the Secretary of Defense, the Chairman of the Federal Deposit Insurance Corporation, the Acting Director of the Federal Housing Finance Agency, the Secretary of Homeland Security, the Secretary of Housing and Urban Development, the Chairman of the National Credit Union Administration, the Comptroller of the Currency, the Secretary of Veterans Affairs, the Director of the Consumer Financial Protection Bureau, and the U.S. Attorney General. The report also is available at no charge on the GAO website at http://www.gao.gov.

If you or your staff have any questions about this report, please contact me at (202) 512-8678 or sciremj@gao.gov. Contact points for our Offices of Congressional Relations and Public Affairs may be found on the last page of this report. GAO staff who made major contributions to this report are listed in appendix XII.

Mathew Scirè
Director
   Financial Markets and
Community Investment

The Honorable Jeff Miller
Chairman
The Honorable Bob Filner
Ranking Member
Committee on Veterans' Affairs
House of Representatives

The Honorable Dan Benishek
House of Representatives

The Honorable Gus Bilirakis
House of Representatives

The Honorable Bruce Braley
House of Representatives

The Honorable Corrine Brown
House of Representatives

The Honorable Jeff Denham
House of Representatives

The Honorable Joe Donnelly
House of Representatives

The Honorable Bill Flores
House of Representatives

The Honorable Tim Huelskamp
House of Representatives

The Honorable Doug Lamborn
House of Representatives

The Honorable Michael Michaud
House of Representatives

The Honorable Silvestre Reyes
House of Representatives

The Honorable Phil Roe
House of Representatives

The Honorable Linda Sanchez
House of Representatives

The Honorable Cliff Stearns
House of Representatives

The Honorable Marlin Stutzman
House of Representatives

Appendix I: Objectives, Scope, and Methodology

Our objectives were to examine (1) what is known about Servicemembers Civil Relief Act (SCRA) eligibility, the number of violations that have occurred, and practices financial institutions use to comply with SCRA; (2) what oversight financial regulators and other federal agencies have taken to help ensure depository institutions' compliance with the act; and (3) actions the Department of Defense (DOD), Department of Homeland Security (DHS), Department of Veterans Affairs (VA), and others have taken to ensure that servicemembers and others are informed of protections provided under the act. With the exception of our regulatory compliance review, the scope of our review includes only SCRA protections related to servicemembers' residential mortgages.

SCRA Compliance

To describe what is known about the practices depository institutions use to comply with SCRA, we interviewed representatives from a non-generalizable sample of four large mortgage servicers and one national consumer credit reporting agency about their SCRA compliance practices and challenges and reviewed relevant policies and procedures. We selected 4 mortgage servicers that were among the 10 largest based on data from the Consolidated Reports of Condition and Income (Call Reports) on the unpaid principal balance of residential mortgages institutions own and service, plus mortgage loans they service on behalf of other institutions, and mortgage servicers that had participated in either the prudential regulators' interagency review of foreclosure policies and practices or the U.S. House of Representatives Committee on Oversight and Government Reform's investigation.[1] We interviewed representatives of financial industry trade associations, including those that represent the mortgage industry, depository institutions with a large military customer base, and the credit reporting industry. We also interviewed officials from DOD's Defense Manpower Data Center, which operates the website that depository institutions and others use to verify the active duty status of servicemembers. To determine what is known about SCRA violations that

---

[1]The Consolidated Reports of Condition and Income (Call Reports) are a primary source of financial data used for the supervision and regulation of banks. They consist of a balance sheet, an income statement, and supporting schedules. The Report of Condition schedules provide details on assets, liabilities, and capital accounts. The Report of Income schedules provide details on income and expenses. Every national bank, state member bank, and insured state nonmember bank is required to file a consolidated Call Report normally as of the close of business on the last calendar day of each calendar quarter. The specific reporting requirements depend upon the size of the bank and whether it has any foreign offices.

have occurred we reviewed letters from 10 large mortgage servicers
written in response to a House of Representatives Committee on
Oversight and Government Reform investigation on mortgage servicers'
SCRA compliance history and practices. We also reviewed data on SCRA
violations found during bank and credit union examinations conducted
from 2007 through 2011 by the prudential regulators—the Board of
Governors of the Federal Reserve System (Federal Reserve), the Federal
Deposit Insurance Corporation (FDIC), the National Credit Union
Administration (NCUA), and the Office of the Comptroller of the Currency
(OCC). We also reviewed available information from legal actions taken
by the Department of Justice (DOJ) against two mortgage servicers for
SCRA violations and a class action settlement against a large mortgage
servicer for SCRA violations. Finally, we reviewed DOJ, Federal Reserve,
and OCC enforcement actions against mortgage servicers for, among
other things, foreclosure documentation problems that require the
mortgage servicers to conduct reviews, which are currently ongoing, to
determine historical SCRA violations.

SCRA Compliance Oversight

To assess the oversight prudential regulators have taken to help ensure
depository institutions' compliance with SCRA, we reviewed their
examination policies and procedures and interviewed agency officials
about their oversight activities related to SCRA. We also reviewed
interagency examination procedures and checklists the regulators
developed in 2009 to aid their oversight of SCRA. To assess the extent to
which prudential regulators examined for SCRA, we selected a stratified
random sample of 160 institutions from the population of all depository
institutions that serviced mortgages as of November 2011 for institutions
regulated by FDIC, Federal Reserve, and OCC, and September 2011 for
institutions regulated by NCUA. We developed a certainty stratum
composed of the 10 largest institutions regulated by each of the four
prudential regulators—FDIC, Federal Reserve, NCUA, and OCC—for a
total of 40 institutions. The remaining 120 institutions comprised an
additional four strata of institutions of varying sizes—one stratum per
prudential regulator. We used the Call Reports to identify mortgage
servicers based on data the institutions reported on the unpaid principal
balance of residential mortgages they own and service, plus mortgage
loans they service on behalf of other institutions.[2] We selected credit

---

[2]We included institutions from all U.S. states and territories.

unions that service mortgage loans using data from the SNL Financial
Database on the unpaid principal balance of real estate loans owned and
serviced, plus those serviced on behalf of other institutions.[3] We
confirmed our use of the relevant mortgage variables with the SNL
Financial Database with NCUA. We excluded any depository institutions
that did not service mortgages. We then used these data to select a
stratified random sample from the population of depository institutions
that service mortgages. While we initially selected a sample of 160
institutions (40 for each regulator), we excluded 8 of the selected
institutions from our analysis. Three institutions regulated by the Federal
Reserve were excluded because they were recently chartered and
therefore had not had an examination. We also excluded five credit
unions because they were state-chartered, meaning that state
supervisory authorities and not NCUA served as the primary regulator for
these institutions. Table 2 provides more detail on the population, sample,
and sample disposition by stratum.

Table 2: Number of Depository Institutions in Sample

	Population	Sample selected	Out of scope	In-scope sample
Largest 10 institutions for each regulator	40	40	0	40
Remaining institutions regulated by FDIC	4,555	30	0	30
Remaining institutions regulated by Federal Reserve	807	30	3	27
Remaining institutions regulated by NCUA	5,280	30	5	25
Remaining institutions regulated by OCC	1,910	30	0	30
Total	**12,592**	**160**	**8**	**152**

Source: GAO analysis of Call Report and SNL Financial Database data.

[3]NCUA maintains a financial reporting system for credit unions separate from the Call
Reports FDIC maintains for depository institutions. Credit unions submit financial reports
to NCUA credit union regulators (also referred to as Call Reports), which are then
compiled into quarterly listings referred to as the 5300 Call Report.

To determine the extent to which prudential regulators included SCRA compliance within the scope of their examinations, we requested SCRA-related examination workpapers, as well as documents examiners prepare to determine the scope of their examinations for all consumer compliance examinations the prudential regulators conducted from 2007 through 2011. We reviewed examinations conducted over a 5-year period because regulatory officials told us that they may not conduct an examination for a particular institution every 12 months, and because SCRA might not be covered in each risk-based examination. We relied on the examination documentation provided to us by the prudential regulators to represent the full universe of examinations that were conducted for each institution in our sample between 2007 and 2011. We did not independently verify that the examination documentation they provided to us represented the full universe of examinations they conducted over this period. We reviewed the documents we received and developed a data collection instrument (DCI) to capture the information we found in the examination documentation in a consistent manner. We determined that a depository institution had received an SCRA compliance review if examination workpapers revealed an SCRA compliance review for any type of loan product covered by the act (for example, residential mortgages, automobile loans, or credit cards loans). We aggregated this examination-level data to the institution level and used the data to produce estimates of the percentage of all institutions for which the prudential regulators included an SCRA compliance review within an examination at least once during the 5-year period. Because we followed a probability procedure based on random selections, our sample of institutions is only one of a large number of samples that we might have drawn. Since each sample could have provided different estimates, we express our confidence in the precision of our particular sample's results as a 95 percent confidence interval (for example, plus or minus 10 percentage points). This is the interval that would contain the actual population value for 95 percent of the samples we could have drawn. For estimates used in this report, we report the 95 percent confidence intervals along with the estimates themselves. We also report percentages based on the 10 largest institutions per regulator. Since these percentages are based on the total population of such institutions, they have no sampling error and consequently confidence intervals are not reported for these percentages.

We reviewed examination workpapers and used our DCI to document the procedures examiners indicated they used to assess SCRA compliance. We only noted the examination procedures for SCRA compliance reviews that involved residential mortgage loans or did not specify the type of loan

product covered. Eighty-three institutions in our sample met these criteria.
SCRA examination procedures for exams that solely focused on other
loan products, such as credit cards and automobile loans, were outside
the scope of our review. We then grouped the data we collected on
examination procedures into four categories:

- *Requests for information from depository institutions.* This includes
  activities such as requests for institutions' internal audit results,
  policies and procedures, SCRA complaints, and lists of SCRA loans. [4]

- *Interviews with depository institution personnel.* This includes
  activities in which examiners interviewed staff at the depository
  institution for information on, among other things, their compliance
  management systems and whether the institution services SCRA
  loans.

- *Assessments of depository institutions' compliance management
  systems.* This category includes instances in which examiners
  documented that they reviewed the quality of depository institutions'
  compliance management systems, such as reviewing institutions'
  SCRA policies and procedures, internal controls, and training
  programs.

- *Testing loan files for SCRA compliance.* This category includes
  activities such as testing a limited or statistical sampling of loans the
  institution identified as SCRA-eligible or conducting more
  comprehensive testing, such as reviewing a statistical sample of loan
  files.

Table 3 provides additional detail on the individual examination activities
that comprise each of these categories.

---

[4]Our review did not identify any institutions that had examinations for SCRA compliance
from 2007 through 2011 that consisted only of requests for information.

Table 3: Examination Activities Identified by GAO for SCRA Compliance Reviews

Category of Activity	Examples of examination activities documented
Requests for information from depository institutions	• Requests for lists of loans the depository institution self-identified as SCRA-eligible • Requests for consumer complaints against the depository institution involving SCRA • Requests for internal audit results regarding SCRA
Interviews with depository institution personnel	• Interviews with depository institution personnel (for example, compliance officers or senior managers) about whether they service any SCRA loans • Interviews with depository institution personnel about internal controls and other measures they take to ensure SCRA compliance

Assessments of depository institutions' compliance management systems	• Reviews of depository institutions' Board of Directors' or Compliance Committee's meeting minutes regarding SCRA
	• Reviews of consumer complaints against a depository institution (either received by the institution or the relevant prudential regulator)
	• Evaluations of the adequacy of depository institutions':
	  • SCRA policies and procedures
	  • self-assessments on foreclosure management policies, particularly those related to SCRA
	  • SCRA compliance training programs
	• Evaluations of the functioning of a depository institution's internal controls related to SCRA
	• Evaluations of the depository institution's internal audit results regarding SCRA
	• Assessments of the depository institution's effort to address previous SCRA violations or deficiencies

Testing loan files for SCRA compliance	• Testing either a limited or a statistical sampling of loans that the depository institution had self-identified as SCRA-eligible • Testing a limited or statistical sampling of a depository institution's entire portfolio of mortgage loans for SCRA compliance

Source: GAO analysis of prudential regulator examination workpapers.

We reviewed prudential regulators' examination guidance and government auditing standards, which note that various activities can provide increasing levels of assurance that reviewed entities are following their stated policies and procedures and that internal controls are functioning. Based on this review, we grouped examiners' documented examination procedures into four categories based on our professional judgment as to the extent to which the examination activities involved verification of assertions made by the depository institution regarding compliance with SCRA. For example, based on our categories, category 1—requests for information from depository institutions—provides the least assurance of SCRA compliance because it does not involve an assessment of compliance, but rather the collection of information. Category 2—interviews with depository institution personnel—also provides less assurance because it relies primarily on assertions provided

by the institution. Whereas category 4—testing of loan files—provides the
greatest assurance of SCRA compliance within our categories because
testing loan files allows examiners to independently verify whether an
institution's compliance procedures are functioning properly and whether
SCRA protections are being appropriately extended to eligible borrowers.
Examination guidance from three of the four prudential regulators cite the
testing of individual loan transactions as the most extensive level of
review for assurance that a depository institution is complying with laws
and regulations. They also indicate that testing a larger sample of loans,
including a statistical sample, provides a fuller assessment of compliance
than testing a limited sample. We placed institutions in each of the four
categories based on the highest level of examination activity conducted
from 2007 through 2011. The figures presented for this analysis are not
generalizable to the population of institutions that service mortgages.

To describe the SCRA compliance oversight activities of other federal
agencies, we reviewed DOJ's policies and procedures for receiving
SCRA referrals and investigating SCRA cases and interviewed agency
officials. We also reviewed DOJ enforcement actions and investigations
that DOJ was able to resolve without filing a court case related to
servicemembers' mortgages from 2007 through 2011. We also reviewed
the SCRA compliance monitoring activities and policies and procedures
of other federal agencies that play a role in the mortgage market. These
agencies include the Federal Housing Administration (FHA), the Federal
Housing Finance Agency (FHFA), and VA. We also reviewed the SCRA
compliance monitoring efforts of two government-sponsored
enterprises—Fannie Mae and Freddie Mac. We reviewed the guidance
these agencies and enterprises provide to mortgage servicers
participating in their programs and interviewed agency officials.

Servicemember Education and Awareness

To determine what actions DOD, DHS, VA, and others have taken to
ensure servicemembers are informed of their SCRA rights, we reviewed
the act to determine what it requires agencies to do and interviewed two
SCRA experts. To describe what actions individual agencies were taking to
inform servicemembers of their rights, we reviewed DOD and DHS policies
and procedures and SCRA training materials and publications, and
interviewed representatives from these agencies, including officials from
DOD's Office of Legal Policy, DHS, and the National Guard Bureau. We
also reviewed DOD's Status of Forces surveys to active duty
servicemembers and members of the reserve components to determine
efforts DOD has taken to assess the effectiveness of its methods of
educating servicemembers about SCRA benefits. We selected six military

installation legal assistance offices (one for the Army, Navy, Marine Corps, and Coast Guard and two for the Air Force) based on a geographic distribution of states with high numbers of foreclosures and large active duty and reservist populations and interviewed legal assistance attorneys who work in these offices to learn how the attorneys teach servicemembers about their SCRA protections and discuss the challenges servicemembers face asserting those protections. The six installations were: Fort Drum, New York; Randolph Air Force Base, San Antonio, Texas; Fort Sam Houston, San Antonio, Texas; Marine Corps Recruit Depot, San Diego, California; Coast Guard 9th District Command Center, Ohio; and Naval Air Station Pensacola, Florida. We reviewed examples of SCRA training and outreach that these offices develop and distribute to servicemembers. To learn about the specific challenges that members of the reserve components face, we also spoke with legal assistance attorneys from the Naval Reserves and the Ohio National Guard who were recommended to us by legal assistance attorneys with whom we spoke.

To determine what actions other agencies, including VA, the Consumer Financial Protection Bureau, and FHA were taking to inform servicemembers and others of SCRA protections, we reviewed notifications they provide to mortgage servicers on SCRA compliance and interviewed officials at these agencies. We also interviewed representatives from the American Bar Association's Legal Assistance for Military Personnel program to learn how they coordinate with legal assistance attorneys and assist servicemembers with SCRA issues. Finally, we interviewed representatives from seven military servicemember groups whose memberships represent a broad population of servicemembers and their families. These groups included the Reserve Officers Association, National Military Family Association, Military Officers Association of America, Air Force Sergeants Association, National Guard Association of the United States, Naval Enlisted Reserve Association, and Retired Enlisted Association.

We conducted this performance audit from August 2011 to July 2012 in accordance with generally accepted government auditing standards. Those standards require that we plan and perform the audit to obtain sufficient, appropriate evidence to provide a reasonable basis for our findings and conclusions based on our audit objectives. We believe that the evidence obtained provides a reasonable basis for our findings and conclusions based on our audit objectives.

Appendix II: Oversight of Mortgage Servicers' Servicemembers Civil Relief Act Compliance

As of June 2012, three federal agency reviews were under way to determine if servicemembers who were eligible for SCRA mortgage-related protections received them. A total of 14 mortgage servicers are involved in these reviews as a result of recent enforcement actions taken by the Office of the Comptroller of the Currency (OCC), the Board of Governors of the Federal Reserve System (Federal Reserve), and the Department of Justice (DOJ). While each review is separate, some overlap exists in the institutions and timeframes being reviewed. However, officials from DOJ told us they are coordinating the reviews to eliminate unnecessary duplication and overlap at institutions. DOJ also completed one review of a mortgage servicer—Saxon Mortgage Services—in May 2012.

Federal Reserve and OCC Enforcement Actions

In response to deficiencies in the foreclosure process that various mortgage servicers publicly announced beginning in September 2010, OCC and the Federal Reserve conducted a coordinated (interagency) on-site review of 14 mortgage servicers to evaluate the adequacy of controls over their foreclosure processes and their policies and procedures for compliance with applicable federal and state laws.[1] This review identified various weaknesses and deficiencies in these mortgage servicers' foreclosure operations, including violations of SCRA. As a result of these reviews, OCC and the Federal Reserve issued consent orders to the 14 mortgage servicers and their affiliates in April 2011, requiring these institutions to make various corrective actions. One of these actions required each of the mortgage servicers to retain a third-party consultant to conduct independent reviews of foreclosure actions that were initiated, pending, or completed on primary residences from January 1, 2009 through December 31, 2010, to identify borrowers who suffered financial injury as a result of errors, misrepresentations, or other deficiencies in

---

[1]The 14 mortgage servicers included in the consent order are Ally Bank/GMAC Bank; Aurora Bank, FSB; Bank of America, N.A.; Citibank, N.A.; EverBank; HSBC Bank, USA, N.A.; JPMorgan Chase Bank, N.A.; MetLife Bank, N.A; OneWest Bank, FSB; PNC Bank, N.A.; Sovereign Bank; SunTrust Bank; U.S. Bank, N.A.; and Wells Fargo Bank, NA. According to OCC and Federal Reserve's report on this interagency review, these 14 institutions represented over two-thirds of the mortgage servicing industry as of the end of 2010. The former Office of Thrift Supervision (OTS)—a prudential regulator—was also involved in the review and resulting enforcement actions. However, the Dodd-Frank Wall Street and Consumer Protection Act of 2010 eliminated the agency effective July 2011 and transferred the supervisory authority for its institutions to the Federal Deposit Insurance Corporation (FDIC), Federal Reserve, and OCC. FDIC participated in this interagency review in a backup role.

foreclosure actions, and to remediate those borrowers, as appropriate. As part of these independent reviews, the consultants are required to review 100 percent of the foreclosure actions during 2009 and 2010 that involved servicemembers who may have been protected under SCRA.

Because examiners reviewed a relatively small number of foreclosure files during the original interagency review, the reviews required by the consent orders are intended to be more comprehensive. The consent orders require the third-party consultants to develop detailed sampling methodologies for identifying foreclosure actions to include in the review. These methodologies are subject to OCC's and the Federal Reserve's approval. OCC officials told us that, in conjunction with DOD and DOJ, they have worked with the third-party consultants to develop a process to access the Department of Defense's Defense Manpower Data Center's database with custom queries in order for the third-party consultants to accurately identify the pool of potential SCRA-eligible borrowers. To supplement the independent reviews, the regulators also required mortgage servicers and consultants to establish an outreach process for borrowers, including servicemembers, who believe they were financially harmed by improper foreclosure practices to request a review of their foreclosure case. These requests for review must be submitted to the mortgage servicers by September 30, 2012. According to officials from OCC and the Federal Reserve, as of May 2012, preliminary results from this review on instances of SCRA noncompliance were not available.[2]

DOJ Enforcement Actions

On May 26, 2011, DOJ settled two cases against Saxon Mortgage Services and BAC Home Loans Servicing for allegations of violations of

---

[2]GAO issued a report on the actions of the regulators and servicers involved in these reviews. See GAO, *Foreclosure Review: Opportunities Exist to Further Enhance Borrower Outreach Efforts*, GAO-12-776 (Washington, D.C.: June 29, 2012). GAO also has ongoing work looking at the actions of the regulators and servicers.

SCRA's foreclosure provision.[3] The consent orders for each of these cases dictated that damages be paid to affected servicemembers and remedial actions be taken by the mortgage servicers. BAC Home Loans Servicing agreed to pay at least $20 million to resolve the lawsuit, and Saxon Mortgage Services agreed to pay at least $2.35 million. The consent orders also required the mortgage servicers to, among other things, (1) implement revised SCRA policies and procedures specifically about querying the Department of Defense's Defense Manpower Data Center database that contains information on servicemembers' active duty status, (2) implement a foreclosure monitoring program, (3) provide SCRA compliance training to all applicable employees, and (4) conduct reviews to identify additional servicemembers who may have had their SCRA rights violated and compensate them. The reviews required by the consent orders included the following:

- Saxon Mortgage Services was required to review all nonjudicial foreclosures conducted from January 1, 2006, through December 31, 2010, to determine compliance with SCRA. This review was completed in May 2012 and a total of 22 servicemembers were identified as having been improperly foreclosed upon.

- BAC Home Loans Servicing is required to conduct reviews for both the foreclosure and interest-rate provisions of SCRA. Specifically, BAC Home Loans Servicing is to review all nonjudicial foreclosures it conducted from January 1, 2006, through December 31, 2010, for SCRA compliance. For the interest-rate review, the consent order required BAC Home Loans Servicing to retain an independent accounting firm to review a statistically valid sample of home mortgage files from January 1, 2008, through December 31, 2010, and issue a report on whether the mortgage servicer appropriately

---

[3]50 U.S.C. App. §533. *United States v. Saxon Mortgage Services Inc. (Northern District of Texas, Dallas Division).* DOJ's complaint alleged that Saxon's conduct violated §533(c) of SCRA and constituted a pattern or practice of foreclosing on servicemembers without court orders during a period of military service, or a period otherwise protected by SCRA. Saxon Mortgage Services, Inc. is a subsidiary of Morgan Stanley. *United States v. BAC Home Loans Servicing, LP f/k/a Countrywide Home Loans Servicing, LP (Central District of California).* DOJ's complaint alleged that BAC Home Loans Servicing's conduct violated §533(c) of SCRA and constituted a pattern or practice of foreclosing on servicemembers without court orders during a period of military service, or a period otherwise protected by SCRA. BAC Home Loans Servicing LP, formerly known as Countrywide Home Loans Servicing LP, is a subsidiary of Bank of America Corporation.

applied interest rates and fees to servicemembers' mortgages as
required by SCRA.

DOJ officials told us that, as of June 2012, the BAC Home Loans
Servicing review is ongoing.

National Mortgage Settlement

In February 2012, DOJ and 49 state attorneys general settled with five of
the largest national mortgage servicers for a variety of improper mortgage
servicing procedures, including allegations of SCRA violations.[4] The $25
billion settlement was one of the largest financial recoveries obtained by
the attorneys general in history and contains a number of provisions
related to SCRA designed to protect servicemembers' rights and to
provide them additional benefits. To resolve allegations of liability that
have not previously been settled, five mortgage servicers—Ally Financial
Inc., Bank of America Corp., Citigroup Inc., JPMorgan Chase Bank, N.A.,
and Wells Fargo & Company—agreed to conduct a full review, overseen
by DOJ's Civil Rights Division, to determine whether any servicemembers
were foreclosed on in violation of SCRA since January 1, 2006.
Additionally, four of the mortgage servicers— Ally Financial Inc., Bank of
America Corp., Citigroup Inc., and Wells Fargo & Company—agreed to
conduct a thorough review of mortgage loans to determine whether any
servicemember, since January 1, 2008, was charged interest in excess of
6 percent after submitting a valid request to lower the interest rate. The
agreement also specifies compensation above the $25 billion settlement
amount for any SCRA foreclosure or interest-rate violations.[5] Compliance

---

[4]The five servicers were Ally Financial Inc./GMAC, Bank of America Corp., Citigroup Inc.,
JPMorgan Chase Bank, N.A.; and Wells Fargo & Company.

[5]Under the settlement agreement, Ally Financial Inc., Bank of America, Citigroup Inc., and
Wells Fargo & Company will be required to provide any servicemember subjected to a
wrongful foreclosure with a payment equal to the servicemember's lost equity, plus
interest, and an additional $116,785 or an amount provided for the same violation under
the review conducted by OCC or the Federal Reserve, whichever is higher. To ensure
consistency with an earlier private settlement, JPMorgan Chase will provide any
servicemember who was a victim of a wrongful foreclosure as a result of a violation of
SCRA either his or her home free and clear of any debt plus compensation for additional
harm or the cash equivalent of the full value of the home at the time of sale plus
compensation for additional harm suffered. Ally Financial Inc., Bank of America, Citigroup
Inc., and Wells Fargo & Company will be required to provide any servicemember who was
wrongfully charged interest in excess of 6 percent with a payment equal to a refund, with
interest, of any amount charged in excess of 6 percent plus triple the amount refunded or
$500, whichever is larger. JPMorgan Chase had already compensated servicemembers
charged excess interest through the earlier private settlement.

with the SCRA provisions of the settlement will be overseen by DOJ's Civil Rights Division. Table 4 summarizes these three reviews.

Table 4: Summary of Ongoing and Completed Federal Agency Reviews of Mortgage Servicers' SCRA Compliance

Review	Description of review	Mortgage servicer	SCRA provision(s) reviewed	Timeframes for mortgages reviewed
OCC and Federal Reserve Consent Orders	Under consent orders issued by OCC and the Federal Reserve, 14 mortgage servicers are required to retain third-party consultants to conduct independent reviews of foreclosure actions to identify borrowers who were financially harmed as a result of certain deficiencies.	• Ally Bank/GMAC Bank • Aurora Bank, FSB • Bank of America, N.A. • Citibank, N.A. • EverBank • HSBC Bank, USA, N.A. • JPMorgan Chase, N.A. • MetLife, N.A. • OneWest Bank, FSB • PNC Bank, N.A. • Sovereign Bank • SunTrust Bank • U.S. Bank, N.A. • Wells Fargo Bank, NA	Foreclosure	2009–2010 (January 1, 2009 through December 1, 2010)
DOJ Consent Orders Saxon Mortgage Services (Morgan Stanley)[a]	Under the consent order, Saxon Mortgage Services was required to review nonjudicial foreclosures (i.e., foreclosures that took place in states that do not require a court order for foreclosure proceedings).	Saxon Mortgage Services, Inc. (a subsidiary of Morgan Stanley)	Foreclosure	2006–2010 (January 1, 2006 through December 31, 2010)
BAC Home Loans Servicing (Bank of America)	Under the consent order, BAC Home Loans Servicing is required to review nonjudicial foreclosures (i.e., foreclosures that took place in states that do not require a court order for foreclosure proceedings).	BAC Home Loans Servicing (a subsidiary of Bank of America)	Foreclosure	2006–2010 (January 1, 2006 through December 31, 2010)

Review	Description of review	Mortgage servicer	SCRA provision(s) reviewed	Timeframes for mortgages reviewed
	Under the consent order, BAC Home Loans Servicing is required to retain an independent accounting firm to review a statistically valid sample of home mortgage files from January 1, 2008, and issue a report on whether the mortgage servicer appropriately applied interest rates and fees to servicemembers' mortgages as required by SCRA.		Interest rate	2008–2010 (January 1, 2008 through December 31, 2010)
National Mortgage Settlement	Five mortgage servicers agreed to conduct a full review, overseen by DOJ's Civil Rights Division, to determine whether any servicemembers were foreclosed on in violation of SCRA.	• Ally Financial Inc. • Bank of America Corp. • Citigroup Inc. • Wells Fargo & Company • JPMorgan Chase Bank, N.A.	Foreclosure	2006–present
	Four mortgage servicers agreed to conduct a thorough review overseen by DOJ's Civil Rights Division of mortgage loans to determine whether any servicemember since January 1, 2008, was charged interest in excess of 6 percent after submitting a valid request to lower the interest rate.	• Ally Financial Inc. • Bank of America Corp. • Citigroup Inc. • Wells Fargo & Company	Interest rate	2008–present

Source: GAO analysis of OCC, Federal Reserve, and DOJ consent orders.

[a]DOJ completed the Saxon Mortgage Servicing Review in May 2012.

Appendix III: Comments from the Department of Homeland Security

U.S. Department of Homeland Security
Washington, D.C. 20528

Homeland Security

July 3, 2012

Mathew Sciré
Director, Financial Markets and Community Investment
U.S. Government Accountability Office
441 G Street, NW
Washington, DC 20548

Re: Draft Report GAO-12-700, "MORTGAGE FORECLOSURES: Regulatory Oversight of Compliance with Servicemembers Civil Relief Act Has Been Limited"

Dear Mr. Sciré:

Thank you for the opportunity to review and comment on this draft report. The U.S. Department of Homeland Security (DHS) appreciates the U.S. Government Accountability Office's (GAO's) work in planning and conducting its review and issuing this report.

The draft report contained four recommendations, only one of which directly involves DHS and with which the Department concurs. Specifically, GAO recommended that the Secretaries of the Army, Air Force, Navy, and Homeland Security:

Recommendation: Assess the effectiveness of their efforts to educate servicemembers on SCRA to determine better ways for making servicemembers aware of their SCRA rights and benefits, including improving the ways in which members of the reserve components obtain such information.

Response: Concur. The Coast Guard strives to keep all its members fully aware of Servicemembers Civil Relief Act (SCRA) benefits and rights and will explore measures to assess effectiveness in the future. Currently, the Coast Guard maintains a service-wide effort to keep its military members (active duty and reserve) fully informed of SCRA rights and benefits. The Coast Guard provides SCRA briefs to all active duty and reserve members upon initial entry into the Service. The Coast Guard Reserve also provides reservists information on SCRA during pre-deployment briefs, as well as during "CG Yellow Ribbon Program" pre-deployment, deployment, de-mobilization; and 30-, 60-, and 90-day post-deployment-reconstitution periods.

Additionally, every Coast Guard servicemember has access to information regarding SCRA benefits and rights through published policy directives on the Coast Guard Intranet, the Coast Guard Judge Advocate General Website, http://www.uscg.mil/legal/la/Legal_Assistance_SCRA.asp, and the Coast Guard Legal Service Command Website, http://www.uscg.mil/lsc/soldiers.asp. Furthermore, formal legal assistance is available through all Coast Guard Legal Offices.

Again, thank you for the opportunity to review and comment on this draft report. Please feel free
to contact me if you have any questions. We look forward to working with you in the future.

Sincerely,

Jim H. Crumpacker
Director
Departmental GAO-OIG Liaison Office

2

Appendix IV: Comments from the Department of Defense

GAO received DOD's letter on July 2, 2012.

PERSONNEL AND
READINESS

OFFICE OF THE UNDER SECRETARY OF DEFENSE
4000 DEFENSE PENTAGON
WASHINGTON, D.C. 20301-4000

Mr. Mathew Scire
Director, Financial Markets and Community Investment
U.S. Government Accountability Office
441 G Street, NW
Washington, DC 20548

Dear Mr. Scire:

This is the Department of Defense (DoD) response to the GAO Draft Report, GAO-12-700, "MORTGAGE FORECLOSURES: Regulatory Oversight of Compliance with Servicemembers Civil Relief Act Has Been Limited," dated June 12, 2012 (GAO Code 250623). As these matters are under my purview as the Director of Legal Policy in the Office of the Under Secretary of Defense for Personnel and Readiness, I have been asked to respond.

The DoD appreciates the depth of the GAO's study, and partially concurs with the report.

In response to the recommendation that the Department Secretaries should assess the effectiveness of their efforts to educate servicemembers on the Servicemembers Civil Relief Act (SCRA) to determine better ways for making servicemembers aware of their SCRA rights and benefits, the DoD partially concurs. The education and protection of our servicemembers is our highest priority, and the DoD continuously evaluates the effectiveness of training our servicemembers on their protections under the SCRA. As such, the DoD is committed to continuing to do so bearing in mind the GAO's recommendations.

Indeed, as I noted in testimony before the Senate Banking Committee on this and other financially-related topics, the DoD is in the process of conducting a study of financial issues affecting the Force. The study will be propounded upon those who work with servicemembers and their families in the field and to elicit the best anecdotal and empirical data with respect to all financial issues affecting those who serve. The survey will inform further DoD efforts.

Furthermore, the DoD will continue to inform our servicemembers—particularly members of the reserve components—of their SCRA rights in a multitude of platforms so as to ensure that all are aware of the protections therein. The DoD constantly seeks to improve communications with our servicemembers on these issues, and will strive to develop methods to better disseminate SCRA information to members of the reserve components.

As for our technical comments, page 37, para 1, reads "As discussed above, SCRA requires that servicemembers receive SCRA training during pre- and post- deployment briefings." This statement is incorrect, and should reflect the language on page 33 to which it refers, which states that the "SCRA requires that servicemembers be informed of the rights and protections available under the SCRA upon entry into the military, during initial orientation training, and, in the cases of members of the reserve components, when called to active duty for a period of more than one year." This clarification will ensure consistency and accuracy regarding servicemember expectations under the SCRA.

We appreciate your interest in and continued support for the men and women of our Armed Forces.

Sincerely,

PAUL E. KANTWILL, Colonel, U.S. Army
Director, Office of Legal Policy

2

GAO Draft Report Dated June 12, 2012

GAO-12-700 (GAO CODE 250623)

"MORTGAGE FORECLOSURES: REGULATORY OVERSIGHT OF COMPLIANCE WITH SERVICEMEMBERS CIVIL RELIEF ACT HAS BEEN LIMITED"

DEPARTMENT OF DEFENSE COMMENTS TO THE GAO RECOMMENDATIONS

RECOMMENDATION 1: The GAO recommends that the Secretaries of the Army, Air Force, and Navy, and Homeland Security should assess the effectiveness of their efforts to educate servicemembers on SCRA to determine better ways for making servicemembers aware of their SCRA rights and benefits, including improving the ways in which members of the reserve components obtain such information.

DoD RESPONSE: The DoD partially concurs. The DoD continuously evaluates the effectiveness of training our servicemembers on their protections under the SCRA, and will continue to do so bearing in mind the GAO's recommendations. The DoD constantly seeks to improve communications with our servicemembers on these issues, and will remain alert to methods to improve not only the dissemination of SCRA information to members of the reserve components, but also to ensure retention of the important benefits allowed.

Appendix V: Comments from the Federal Deposit Insurance Corporation

Federal Deposit Insurance Corporation
550 17th Street NW, Washington, D.C. 20429-9990   Division of Depositor and Consumer Protection

July 2, 2012

Mathew J. Scirè
Director
Financial Markets and Community Investment
U.S. Government Accountability Office
441 G Street, NW
Washington, DC 20548

Dear Mr. Scirè:

The FDIC appreciates the opportunity to comment on the GAO report *Mortgage Foreclosures: Regulatory Oversight of Compliance with Servicemembers Civil Relief Act Has Been Limited.* The FDIC takes seriously our responsibility to examine FDIC supervised institutions for compliance with the requirements of the Servicemembers Civil Relief Act (SCRA). As noted in the report, the FDIC performs risk-focused consumer compliance examinations that include SCRA for virtually all of our institutions during the period. Through our supervisory efforts, the FDIC identified a number of SCRA violations and ensured institutions implemented appropriate corrective actions to meet the obligations under the statute.

During the time period of the 2007-2011, the FDIC issued FIL 83-2007 http://www.fdic.gov/news/news/financial/2007/fil07083.html to FDIC-supervised institutions to highlight the effective date and major provisions of the Talent Amendment as well as other protections afforded to service personnel under the Servicemembers Civil Relief Act. In addition, the agencies issued Interagency Guidance on Mortgage Servicing Practices Concerning Military Homeowners with Permanent Change of Station Orders on June 21, 2012.

The report states that interviews with depository institution personnel "provides the least assurance of SCRA compliance" because the examiner is required to "rely" on assertions provided by the employees. The FDIC believes that examiner interviews with bank employees serve as an effective tool for assessing compliance with consumer protection laws and regulations. Examiners are trained to ask open-ended questions to determine whether the responsible institution employees know and understand the law and effectively implement the bank policies. As such, interviews are often used to verify that the bank is conducting sufficient employee training and is enforcing its policies and procedures.

The report further notes that the best method for determining SCRA compliance would be to perform random testing of all mortgage loans. The FDIC agrees that testing a representative sample of loans for compliance with SCRA is an effective tool to assess compliance with SCRA for large mortgage servicers.

Page – 2

The FDIC appreciates the GAO's careful review of regulators' oversight of SCRA and remains committed to continuing our efforts to ensure FDIC-supervised institutions comply with these important protections for servicemembers. Please contact Megan Becker, Management Analyst, Division of Finance - Corporate Management Control, at 703-562-2627 with any questions you may have.

Sincerely,

Mark Pearce
Director
Division of Depositor and Consumer Protection

Appendix VI: Comments from the Board of Governors of the Federal Reserve System

BOARD OF GOVERNORS
OF THE
FEDERAL RESERVE SYSTEM
WASHINGTON, D. C. 20551

SANDRA F. BRAUNSTEIN
DIRECTOR
DIVISION OF CONSUMER
AND COMMUNITY AFFAIRS

June 29, 2012

Mr. Mathew Scirè
Director, Financial Markets and Community Investment
U.S. Government Accountability Office
441 G Street, NW
Washington, DC 20548

Dear Mr. Scirè:

Thank you for the opportunity to comment on the draft report entitled "Mortgage Foreclosures: Regulatory Oversight of Compliance with Servicemembers Civil Relief Act Has Been Limited." The Federal Reserve is committed to ensuring appropriate financial protections for servicemembers whose active duty military service can present challenges to meeting financial obligations. As noted in the report, the Federal Reserve examined for SCRA compliance 92.7 percent of state member banks in your sample within the review period of 2007-2011.

The report also notes that the Federal Reserve and the OCC issued consent orders to 14 large mortgage servicers in April 2011 that require the servicers to take a number of actions. Among other requirements, the servicers must engage independent consultants to conduct a review of loan files to identify borrowers who suffered financial injury as a result of wrongful foreclosures or other deficiencies and provide remediation to those harmed borrowers. The Federal Reserve is requiring the independent consultants to include in the review all files for particular categories of borrowers who we have determined present a significant risk of being financially injured in the foreclosure process. Any borrower who falls into any one of those categories must receive an independent foreclosure review. The categories for mandatory review include all mortgages in the mortgage foreclosure process in 2009 or 2010 involving members of the military who were covered by the Servicemembers Civil Relief Act.

In addition, on February 9, 2012, the Board announced monetary sanctions against five banking organizations totaling $766.5 million for engaging in unsafe and unsound practices in their mortgage loan servicing and processing. These monetary sanctions are based on the same deficiencies that the servicers were required to correct through the action plans under the April 2011 enforcement actions referred to above. The amount of the sanctions takes into account the maximum amount prescribed for unsafe and unsound practices under applicable statutory limits, the comparative severity of each institution's misconduct, and the comparative size of each institution's foreclosure activities.

The draft report includes two recommendations to the Federal Reserve and other federal financial regulators. The first recommendation is that regulators take steps to increase the

Mr. Mathew Sciré
June 29, 2012   2

frequency with which examiners conduct mortgage loan file testing and employ testing methods that provide greater assurance of compliance with SCRA. The report notes that examiners can choose from different types of testing, including interviews with financial institution management, review of the institution's compliance management system, and testing of individual loan files. GAO found that, in most instances, the loans examiners tested were limited to a sample of loans that the financial institution had identified as SCRA-eligible. The Federal Reserve employs a risk-based examination methodology that incorporates all three types of testing noted in the report. For purposes of evaluating a financial institution's compliance with SCRA, Federal Reserve examiners apply interagency examination procedures to test the sufficiency of the institution's program for ensuring its employees provide appropriate protections to active duty servicemembers. The Federal Reserve will work with its federal financial regulatory agency counterparts to consider appropriate ways to update those interagency examination procedures.

The report's second recommendation is that the agencies with oversight responsibility for SCRA compliance (the Comptroller of the Currency, the Board of Governors of the Federal Reserve System, the Federal Deposit Insurance Corporation, the National Credit Union Administration, the Federal Housing Finance Administration, the Department of Housing and Urban Development, and the Department of Veteran Affairs) explore options to share information related to SCRA compliance oversight. The Federal Reserve agrees that additional interagency collaboration related to SCRA trends and emerging risks may be appropriate and useful in improving supervisory practices related to SCRA compliance. As an example of this collaboration, the Federal Reserve is currently planning an interagency servicemembers financial protection webinar for financial industry participants. The webinar is planned to include panelists from the federal financial supervisory agencies and representatives from other agencies with responsibility for SCRA. In addition, we will explore other opportunities to share information with other federal regulators consistent with this recommendation.

We appreciate the professionalism of the GAO's review team in conducting this survey and for the opportunity to provide these comments to the draft report.

Sincerely,

Appendix VII: Comments from the Federal Housing Finance Agency

Federal Housing Finance Agency

Constitution Center
400 7th Street, S.W.
Washington, D.C. 20024
Telephone: (202) 649-3800
Facsimile: (202) 649-1071
www.fhfa.gov

July 6, 2012

Mr. Mathew J. Scire
Director
Financial Markets and Community Investment
Government Accountability Office (GAO)
441 G Street, NW
Washington, DC 20548

Dear Mr. Scire:

Thank you for the opportunity to review and comment on the Government Accountability Office (GAO) Report, *Mortgage Foreclosures: Regulatory Oversight of Compliance with Servicemembers Civil Relief Act Has Been Limited.*

Based on its review, GAO concluded that there currently is not routine sharing of Servicemembers Civil Relief Act (SCRA) compliance information among the federal depository institution regulators, FHA, VA and FHFA, although there are some existing mechanisms for sharing information that could be used or expanded. GAO has recommended that the agencies, including FHFA, should explore options to utilize existing mechanisms or develop new ones to improve interagency information sharing relating to SCRA compliance oversight. FHFA accepts this recommendation and will implement it as described below.

FHFA believes it is critical to work with other supervisory agencies to support U.S. military homeowners, as reflected by coordinated policy decisions regarding short sale relief announced recently by agency leaders. FHFA agrees that increased information sharing among supervisors of mortgage lending industry participants, such as the government-sponsored enterprises, could assist in identifying potential compliance problems and in some cases could improve the identification of SCRA violations. Collaboration among supervisors contributes to consistent and effective oversight of compliance by supervised entities and to the identification of emerging risks and compliance concerns.

As noted in GAO's report, FHFA currently has formal mechanisms in place to permit interagency information sharing in many instances. FHFA has written memoranda of understanding (MOUs) with various agencies that provide channels for disclosure of confidential

Page 2

supervisory information with appropriate confidentiality protections. As a relatively new agency, FHFA is still in the process of developing and refining these formal channels through which information can be exchanged with other supervisors. FHFA's supervision function will consider whether the existing MOUs are sufficient or should be expanded to cover more types of information or more agencies to broaden information sharing on issues of supervisory concern, including SCRA compliance.

In addition to formal channels, FHFA has the ability to initiate or respond to supervisory inquiries on an informal basis, for example, by letter agreements. FHFA supervision will consider whether existing protocols meet supervisory needs, or whether compliance oversight would be improved by development of processes for more frequent, routine communications with supervisors of other market participants subject to mortgage lending compliance requirements.

If you have any questions, please do not hesitate to contact me.

Sincerely,

Jon D. Greenlee
Deputy Director
Division of Enterprise Regulation

Appendix VIII: Comments from the Department of Housing and Urban Development

U.S. DEPARTMENT OF HOUSING AND URBAN DEVELOPMENT
WASHINGTON, DC 20410-8000

ASSISTANT SECRETARY FOR HOUSING-
FEDERAL HOUSING COMMISSIONER

JUL 3 2012

Mr. Mathew J. Scirè
Director
Financial Markets and Community Investment
Government Accountability Office
441 G Street, NW
Washington, DC 20548-0001

Dear Mr. Scirè:

Thank you for the opportunity to comment on the draft GAO -12-700 report entitled, "Mortgage Foreclosures: Regulatory Oversight of Compliance with Servicemembers Civil Relief Act Has Been Limited." This letter conveys HUD's response to the audit. During a conference call on May 15, 2012, FHA's Office of Lender Activities and Program Compliance provided technical comments regarding Servicemembers Civil Relief Act (SCRA) to GAO.

With regard to the recommendations found in the report, FHA agrees with the GAO's recommendation and its specific response is listed below.

Recommendation:

Additionally, to increase agencies' awareness of potential problems with SCRA compliance, the Comptroller of the Currency, the Chairman of the Board of Governors of the Federal Reserve System, the Chairman of the Federal Deposit Insurance Corporation, and Chairman of the National Credit Union Administration, the Acting Director of the Federal Housing Finance Administration, the Secretary of Housing and Urban Development, and the Secretary Veterans Affairs should explore options to utilize existing mechanisms or develop new ones to share information related to SCRA compliance Oversight.

HUD Response:

FHA concurs with the sentiment that it is critical to have interagency collaboration. FHA also agrees that it should participate in agencies' discussions to explore options to utilize existing mechanisms or develop new ones to share information related to SCRA compliance. However, since FHA does not have responsibility for overseeing SCRA, it would assume a participatory role vs. a leadership role. Further, we think that such collaboration should not be limited to SCRA compliance, but should be broad enough in scope to include all of our mutual interests the area of single family housing.

www.hud.gov   espanol.hud.gov

We appreciate the efforts of the GAO to review our compliance with SCRA and suggest recommendation for interagency collaboration to strengthen our regulatory compliance oversight of mortgage foreclosures related to SCRA.

Sincerely,

Carol J. Galante
Acting Assistant Secretary for Housing
Federal Housing Commissioner

National Credit Union Administration
June 25, 2012

Mathew Scire
Director, Financial Markets and Community Investment
United States Government Accountability Office
441 G Street NW
Washington, DC 20548

Dear Mr. Scire:

Thank you for the opportunity to comment on the draft report *Mortgage Foreclosures: Regulatory Oversight of Compliance with Servicemembers Civil Relief Act Has Been Limited* (GAO-12-700). In your report, you recommend the National Credit Union Administration (NCUA) and other federal financial regulators conduct testing of foreclosure files and as applicable, other mortgage loan files, and employ testing methods that provide greater assurance that mortgage servicers are complying with the Servicemembers Civil Relief Act (SCRA). You also recommend the NCUA and other federal financial regulators explore options to use existing mechanisms or develop new ones to share information related to SCRA compliance oversight and increase our awareness of potential compliance problems.

We believe your conclusions are reasonable and consistent with your findings. As you note in your report, testing is an effective monitoring technique, and additional testing of loan files during examinations would provide greater assurance of SCRA compliance. For the past several years, we have been improving our examination process to meet the demands of the current economic environment. In 2009, the NCUA Board approved the creation of the Office of Consumer Protection (OCP) to demonstrate the importance NCUA places on consumer protection and raise the profile of this function. One of OCP's responsibilities is conducting fair lending examinations at federal credit unions nationwide. Starting with our 2011 fair lending examinations, staff separate from our regional, safety and soundness examiners review the lending practices of federal credit unions to ensure compliance with consumer protection laws, including SCRA.

Along with testing during our fair lending examinations, NCUA has incorporated reviews for SCRA compliance in our analysis and investigations of member complaints. Specifically, our online member complaint form includes fields where credit union members can indicate their military affiliation. Additionally, when the SCRA is implicated during staff's review of circumstances involved in a member complaint, we verify the complainant's military status, notify the federal credit union of the potential SCRA compliance risks, and instruct the credit union to analyze and take corrective action on the matter in light of the SCRA.

Our agency uses tools developed by interagency groups as a part of our supervision and compliance programs. Specifically, many of our examination procedures, especially the procedures addressing consumer compliance, are prescribed by the

1775 Duke Street - Alexandria, VA 22314-3428 - 703-518-6300

Mathew Scire
June 25, 2012
Page 2

Federal Financial Institutions Examination Council (FFIEC).[1] Additionally, NCUA uses
our participation in the FFIEC and other interagency working groups, such as the Task
Force on Fair Lending[2], to share information regarding the supervision of financial
institutions and compliance concerns. We are currently sharing information with the
Consumer Financial Protection Bureau regarding consumer compliance oversight and
working with the federal financial regulators to develop tools to facilitate information
sharing. Most recently, NCUA joined the other federal financial regulators to issue
guidance regarding mortgage servicer practices that might pose risks to homeowners
who are serving in the military.

As our agency advances its consumer protection initiatives, we will continue to
encourage credit unions to consistently demonstrate best practices in mortgage lending
and to pay particular attention to the SCRA. We will use your report as a benchmark
when evaluating our supervision practices and working with other regulators to ensure
prudent regulatory oversight.

We appreciate the opportunity to comment and commend the professionalism of your
staff throughout the audit process.

Sincerely,

David Marquis
Executive Director

---

[1] The Federal Financial Institutions Examination Council (FFIEC) is a formal interagency body
empowered to prescribe uniform principles, standards, and report forms for the federal examination of
financial institutions by the Board of Governors of the Federal Reserve System (FRB), the Federal
Deposit Insurance Corporation (FDIC), the National Credit Union Administration (NCUA), the Office of the
Comptroller of the Currency (OCC), the Consumer Financial Protection Bureau (CFPB), and State Liaison
Committee to promote uniformity in the supervision of financial institutions.
[2] The Task Force on Fair Lending is a formal interagency group comprised of the Department of Housing
and Urban Development, Department of Justice, CFPB, FDIC, Federal Housing Finance Agency, FRB,
Federal Trade Commission, NCUA, and OCC.

Appendix X: Comments from the Office of the Comptroller of the Currency

Comptroller of the Currency
Administrator of National Banks

Washington, DC 20219

July 9, 2012

Mr. Mathew Scirè
Director, Financial Markets and Community Investment
United States Government Accountability Office
Washington, DC 20548

Dear Mr. Scirè:

The Office of the Comptroller of the Currency (OCC), has reviewed your draft report titled "Mortgage Foreclosures: Regulatory Oversight of Compliance with Servicemembers Civil Relief Act Has Been Limited" (Report). Your Report responds to Congressional requests to examine various aspects of federal oversight of compliance with the Servicemembers Civil Relief Act (SCRA).

The Report included the following findings: (1) of the institutions reviewed for SCRA compliance, only about half received examinations that involved testing of compliance by reviewing loan files; (2) examiners only reviewed loans identified by the institution as involving servicemembers and had not independently selected a statistical sample of loans files; and (3) while there are various federal agencies and institution regulators involved in SCRA compliance oversight, these groups do not share information among themselves.

To help ensure institution compliance and effective oversight by regulators, the Report recommends that institution regulators increase the frequency with which examiners conduct testing of foreclosure and other mortgage loan files, and employ testing methods that provide a greater assurance that mortgage servicers are complying with the SCRA. The Report also recommends that federal agencies and institution regulators explore options to utilize existing mechanisms or develop new ones to share information related to SCRA compliance oversight.

We agree with the Report recommendations and will update our examination guidelines to ensure that a review of SCRA compliance is conducted during each supervisory cycle for OCC-regulated institutions. The review will include the testing of loan files selected using an appropriate methodology to assess compliance with the SCRA. The OCC will also continue to be an active member of the Federal Financial Institutions Examination Council (FFIEC) Task Force on Consumer Compliance, an interagency organization that works collectively to develop examiner guidance, examination procedures, and discuss emerging risks or trends identified regarding new products/services. FFIEC SCRA examination procedures were developed and issued in 2009. As part of an interagency effort to provide guidance to the industry, the OCC and other federal regulators recently issued guidance on Mortgage Servicing Practices Concerning Military Homeowners with Permanent Change of Station Orders. Additionally, the

OCC, the other prudential regulators, and the Consumer Financial Protection Bureau (CFPB) signed a Memorandum of Understanding on Supervisory Coordination that outlines the coordination of examinations and the sharing of compliance oversight information, including SCRA.

We appreciate the opportunity to comment on the draft Report. If you need additional information, please contact John Lyons, Senior Deputy Comptroller for Bank Supervision Policy and Chief National Bank Examiner, at 202-874-2870.

Sincerely,

Thomas J. Curry
Comptroller of the Currency

-2-

Appendix XI: Comments from the Department of Veterans Affairs

DEPARTMENT OF VETERANS AFFAIRS
Washington DC 20420

July 6, 2012

Mr. Mathew Scirè
Director, Financial Markets and
  Community Investment
U.S. Government Accountability Office
441 G Street, NW
Washington, DC 20548

Dear Mr. Scirè:

The Department of Veterans Affairs (VA) has reviewed the Government Accountability Office's (GAO) draft report, *"MORTGAGE FORECLOSURES: Regulatory Oversight of Compliance with Servicemembers Civil Relief Act Has Been Limited"* (GAO-12-700), and concurs with both recommendations.

The enclosure specifically addresses GAO's recommendations and contains a technical comment. VA appreciates the opportunity to comment on your draft report.

Sincerely,

John R. Gingrich
Chief of Staff

Enclosure

Enclosure

Department of Veterans Affairs (VA) Comments to
Government Accountability Office (GAO) Draft Report
*"MORTGAGE FORECLOSURES: Regulatory Oversight of Compliance
with Servicemembers Civil Relief Act Has Been Limited"*
(GAO-12-700)

GAO Recommendation 1: To help ensure that VA assists servicemembers with remaining in their homes and avoiding foreclosure, the Secretary of Veterans Affairs should ensure that a review for SCRA compliance is included in the department's new mortgage servicer monitoring program and that additional steps to assess SCRA compliance are taken by VA staff during its Adequacy of Servicing reviews and while conducting supplemental servicing.

VA Response: Concur. One emphasis of VA's Home Loan Program is to ensure all Veterans and Servicemembers receive every opportunity to retain their homes or avoid foreclosure. VA accomplishes this by advocating for Veterans to make sure they are aware of their protections under SCRA. This includes sending letters and talking personally to Veteran borrowers in default to advise them of SCRA protections, handing out "quick books" detailing SCRA provisions at military and homeowner-focused events, and providing a SCRA Web banner on VA's Home Loan Web page detailing all of the SCRA mortgage protections. VA will revalidate and as necessary, revise its focus and procedures to ensure Veteran borrowers are receiving all SCRA protections to which they are entitled. VA is committed to assisting Veteran borrowers during times of financial hardship and to appropriately notify DOJ and other stakeholder agencies/regulators of any identified violations. As noted in the report, the Department of Justice (DOJ) has explicit authority to enforce compliance with SCRA.

Regarding the recommendation to ensure that a review for SCRA compliance is included in the Department's new mortgage servicer-monitoring program, VA will include in its mortgage servicer-monitoring program a review, which ensures that, as a part of servicers' loss mitigation efforts, servicers acted to appropriately afford SCRA-eligible borrowers the mortgage protections available to them under SCRA. If violations of SCRA mortgage provisions are discovered, VA will also act to appropriately notify DOJ and other stakeholder agencies/regulators of those violations. VA expects to implement the enhancement to the servicer-monitoring program by September 30, 2012.

Regarding the recommendation that additional steps to assess SCRA compliance are taken by VA staff during its Adequacy of Servicing reviews and while conducting supplemental servicing, VA will incorporate additional steps to assess whether the servicer acted to appropriately afford SCRA-eligible borrowers with the mortgage protections available to them under SCRA. If violations of SCRA mortgage provisions are discovered, VA will also act to appropriately notify DOJ and other stakeholder agencies/regulators of those violations. VA expects to have these additional Adequacy of Servicing review steps implemented by August 1, 2012.

1

Department of Veterans Affairs (VA) Comments to
Government Accountability Office (GAO) Draft Report
*"MORTGAGE FORECLOSURES: Regulatory Oversight of Compliance
with Servicemembers Civil Relief Act Has Been Limited"*
(GAO-12-700)

GAO Recommendation 2: To increase agencies' awareness of potential problems
with SCRA compliance, the Comptroller of the Currency, the Chairman of the Board of
Governors of the Federal Reserve System, the Chairman of the Federal Deposit
Insurance Corporation, and Chairman of the National Credit Union Administration, the
Acting Director of the Federal Housing Finance Administration, the Secretary of Housing
and Urban Development, and the Secretary Veterans Affairs should explore options to
utilize existing mechanisms or develop new ones to share information related to SCRA
compliance oversight.

VA Response: Concur. VA will collaborate with the noted government entities and
explore options to utilize existing mechanisms or develop new ones to share information
related to SCRA oversight.

2

Appendix XII: GAO Contact and Staff Acknowledgments

GAO Contact	Mathew J. Scirè, (202) 512-8678, or sciremj@gao.gov
Staff Acknowledgments	In addition to the individual named above, Cody Goebel, Assistant Director; Meghana Acharya; Rachel Batkins; Rudy Chatlos; Christine Houle; John McGrail; Mark Ramage; and Jennifer Schwartz made key contributions to this report.

GAO's Mission	The Government Accountability Office, the audit, evaluation, and investigative arm of Congress, exists to support Congress in meeting its constitutional responsibilities and to help improve the performance and accountability of the federal government for the American people. GAO examines the use of public funds; evaluates federal programs and policies; and provides analyses, recommendations, and other assistance to help Congress make informed oversight, policy, and funding decisions. GAO's commitment to good government is reflected in its core values of accountability, integrity, and reliability.
Obtaining Copies of GAO Reports and Testimony	The fastest and easiest way to obtain copies of GAO documents at no cost is through GAO's website (www.gao.gov). Each weekday afternoon, GAO posts on its website newly released reports, testimony, and correspondence. To have GAO e-mail you a list of newly posted products, go to www.gao.gov and select "E-mail Updates."
Order by Phone	The price of each GAO publication reflects GAO's actual cost of production and distribution and depends on the number of pages in the publication and whether the publication is printed in color or black and white. Pricing and ordering information is posted on GAO's website, http://www.gao.gov/ordering.htm. Place orders by calling (202) 512-6000, toll free (866) 801-7077, or TDD (202) 512-2537. Orders may be paid for using American Express, Discover Card, MasterCard, Visa, check, or money order. Call for additional information.
Connect with GAO	Connect with GAO on Facebook, Flickr, Twitter, and YouTube. Subscribe to our RSS Feeds or E-mail Updates. Listen to our Podcasts. Visit GAO on the web at www.gao.gov.
To Report Fraud, Waste, and Abuse in Federal Programs	Contact: Website: www.gao.gov/fraudnet/fraudnet.htm E-mail: fraudnet@gao.gov Automated answering system: (800) 424-5454 or (202) 512-7470
Congressional Relations	Katherine Siggerud, Managing Director, siggerudk@gao.gov, (202) 512-4400, U.S. Government Accountability Office, 441 G Street NW, Room 7125, Washington, DC 20548
Public Affairs	Chuck Young, Managing Director, youngc1@gao.gov, (202) 512-4800 U.S. Government Accountability Office, 441 G Street NW, Room 7149 Washington, DC 20548

Please Print on Recycled Paper.